THE 9/11 REPORT

THE 9/11 REPORT

A Graphic Adaptation

by

Sid Jacobson and Ernie Colón

VIKING

PUBLISHED BY THE PENGUIN GROUP
PENGUIN BOOKS LTD, 80 STRAND, LONDON WC2R 0RL, ENGLAND
PENGUIN GROUP (USA) INC., 375 HUDSON STREET, NEW YORK, NEW YORK 10014, USA
PENGUIN GROUP (CANADA), 90 EGLINTON AVENUE EAST, SUITE 700, TORONTO, ONTARIO, CANADA M4P 2Y3
(A DIVISION OF PEARSON PENGUIN CANADA INC.)
PENGUIN IRELAND, 25 ST STEPHEN'S GREEN, DUBLIN 2, IRELAND (A DIVISION OF PENGUIN BOOKS LTD)
PENGUIN GROUP (AUSTRALIA), 250 CAMBERWELL ROAD,
CAMBERWELL, VICTORIA 3124, AUSTRALIA (A DIVISION OF PEARSON AUSTRALIA GROUP PTY LTD)
PENGUIN BOOKS INDIA PVT LTD, 11 COMMUNITY CENTRE,
PANCHSHEEL PARK, NEW DELHI—-110 017, INDIA
PENGUIN GROUP (NZ), CNR AIRBORNE AND ROSEDALE ROADS, ALBANY,
AUCKLAND 1310, NEW ZEALAND (A DIVISION OF PEARSON NEW ZEALAND LTD)
PENGUIN BOOKS (SOUTH AFRICA) (PTY) LTD, 24 STURDEE AVENUE,
ROSEBANK, JOHANNESBURG 2196, SOUTH AFRICA

PENGUIN BOOKS LTD, REGISTERED OFFICES: 80 STRAND, LONDON WC2R 0RL, ENGLAND

WWW.PENGUIN.COM

FIRST PUBLISHED IN THE UNITED STATES OF AMERICA BY HILL AND WANG,
A DIVISION OF FARRAR, STRAUS AND GIROUX 2006
FIRST PUBLISHED IN GREAT BRITAIN BY VIKING 2006
1

COPYRIGHT © CASTLEBRIDGE ENTERPRISES, INC., 2006
FOREWORD COPYRIGHT © 2006 BY THOMAS H. KEAN AND LEE H. HAMILTON
TEXT ADAPTED FROM THE 9/11 REPORT,
BY THE NATIONAL COMMISSION ON TERRORIST ATTACKS ON THE UNITED STATES

THE MORAL RIGHT OF THE AUTHOR HAS BEEN ASSERTED

PRINTED IN THE UNITED STATES OF AMERICA BY R. R. DONNELLEY

A CIP CATALOGUE RECORD FOR THIS BOOK IS AVAILABLE FROM THE BRITISH LIBRARY

TRADE PAPERBACK
ISBN-13: 978-0-670-91673-3
ISBN-10: 0-670-91673-0

THIS BOOK IS DEDICATED TO THE MEMORY OF THOSE
WHO LOST THEIR LIVES IN THE TRAGEDY OF 9/11.
WE HOPE THIS BOOK CAN HELP THE REST OF US
TO UNDERSTAND BETTER WHAT HAPPENED THAT DAY AND
IN THE YEARS LEADING UP TO IT.

CONTENTS

FOREWORD

IT WAS THE GOAL OF THE COMMISSION TO TELL THE STORY OF 9/11 IN A
WAY THAT THE AMERICAN PEOPLE COULD READ AND UNDERSTAND. WE
FELT STRONGLY THAT ONE OF THE MOST IMPORTANT AND TRAGIC EVENTS
IN OUR NATION'S HISTORY NEEDED TO BE ACCESSIBLE TO ALL. OUR GOAL
IN THE 9/11 COMMISSION REPORT WAS NOT ONLY TO INFORM OUR FELLOW
CITIZENS ABOUT HISTORY BUT ALSO TO ENERGIZE AND ENGAGE THEM ON
BEHALF OF REFORM AND CHANGE, TO MAKE OUR COUNTRY SAFER AND
MORE SECURE.

FOR THIS REASON, WE ARE PLEASED TO HAVE THE OPPORTUNITY TO
BRING THE WORK OF THE 9/11 COMMISSION TO THE ATTENTION OF A NEW
SET OF READERS. WE COMMEND THE TALENTED GRAPHIC ARTISTS OF
THIS EDITION FOR THEIR CLOSE ADHERENCE TO THE FINDINGS,
RECOMMENDATIONS, SPIRIT, AND TONE OF THE ORIGINAL COMMISSION
REPORT. THEIR ADAPTATION CONVEYS MUCH OF THE INFORMATION
CONTAINED IN THE ORIGINAL REPORT. WE BELIEVE THAT YOU WILL FIND
THE STORY OF 9/11 A GRIPPING ONE, WHETHER IN NARRATIVE OR
PICTORIAL FORM.

WE HOPE READERS OF ALL AGES, ESPECIALLY THOSE UNFAMILIAR WITH
THE ORIGINAL REPORT, FIND THAT THESE PAGES ENCOURAGE THEM TO
LEARN MORE ABOUT THE EVENTS OF 9/11 . WE WOULD BE DELIGHTED IF
THIS PUBLICATION LED TO ADDITIONAL NATIONAL CONVERSATION ABOUT
THE RECOMMENDATIONS OF THE 9/11 COMMISSION REPORT, AND THE
EXTENT TO WHICH THEY HAVE BEEN IMPLEMENTED.

THE SAFETY AND SECURITY OF OUR COUNTRY REQUIRE A WELL-
INFORMED PUBLIC TO HOLD ITS ELECTED LEADERS TO ACCOUNT. HAVE
OUR LEADERS DONE ALL THAT THEY CAN AND SHOULD TO PROTECT THE
AMERICAN PEOPLE? IT IS UP TO EACH OF US TO INSIST THAT THEY DO. AS
WE STATED IN OUR ORIGINAL PREFACE TO THE COMMISSION REPORT, WE
HOPE THAT THIS GRAPHIC VERSION WILL ENCOURAGE OUR FELLOW
CITIZENS TO STUDY, REFLECT--AND ACT.

THOMAS H. KEAN   LEE H. HAMILTON
CHAIR   VICE CHAIR
THE 9/11 COMMISSION   THE 9/11 COMMISSION

JUNE 2006

THE 9/11 REPORT

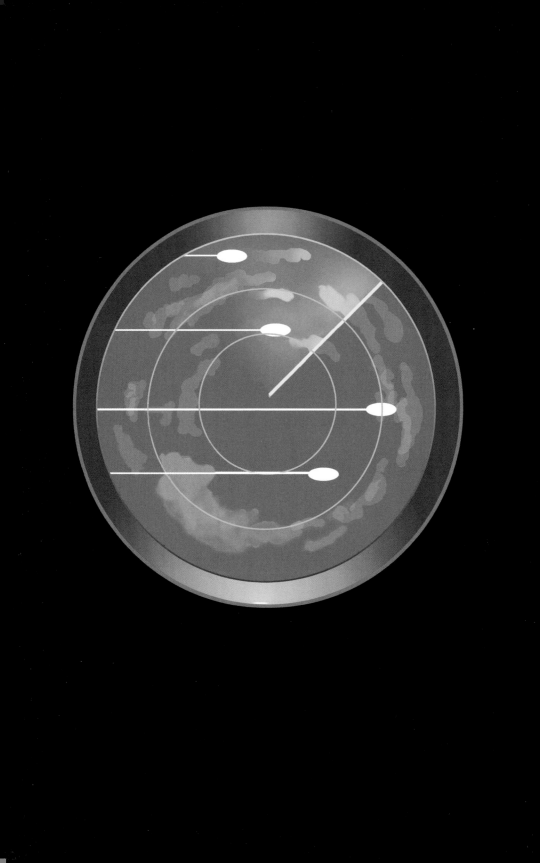

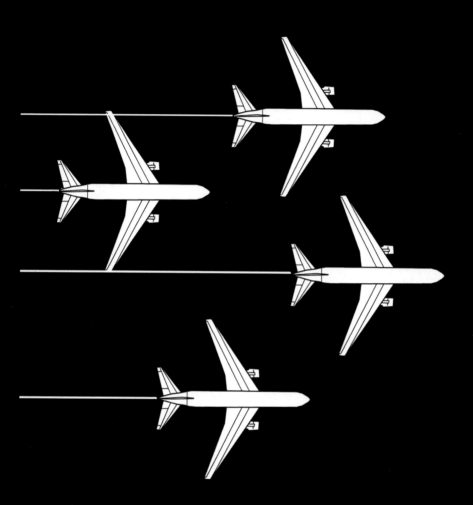

Chapter 1:

"WE HAVE SOME PLANES..."

AMERICAN AIRLINES FLIGHT 11

SATAM AL SUQAMI   WAIL AL SHEHRI   WALEED AL SHEHRI   ABDUL AZIZ AL OMARI   MOHAMED ATTA PILOT

UNITED AIRLINES FLIGHT 175

MARWAN AL SHEHHI PILOT   FAYEZ BANIHAMMAD   AHMED AL GHAMDI   HAMZA AL GHAMDI   MOHAND AL SHEHRI

AMERICAN AIRLINES FLIGHT 77

NAWAF AL HAZMI   MAJED MOQED   HANI HANJOUR PILOT   KHALID AL MIHDHAR   SALEM AL HAZMI

UNITED AIRLINES FLIGHT 93

AHMED AL NAMI   SAEED AL GHAMDI   ZIAD JARRAH PILOT   AHMAD AL HAZNAWI

Inside the Four Flights

BEFORE 8 O'CLOCK ON TUESDAY, SEPTEMBER 11, 2001, A PLEASANT AND CLOUDLESS MORNING IN BOSTON, TWO PLANES, BOTH BOEING 767s, WERE ABOUT TO TAKE OFF FROM LOGAN AIRPORT...

...AND CHANGE THE HISTORY OF THIS NATION.

FIVE ARAB NATIONALS SCHEDULED TO BOARD AMERICAN AIRLINES FLIGHT 11, A 7:45 FLIGHT TO LOS ANGELES...

...WERE PASSED THROUGH WITHOUT INCIDENT.

PILLOW, ANYONE?

IN ANOTHER LOGAN TERMINAL, FIVE OTHER ARAB NATIONALS BOARDED UNITED FLIGHT 175, AN 8 O'CLOCK FLIGHT TO LOS ANGELES, AND TOOK THEIR SEATS, ALSO WITHOUT INCIDENT.

BY 8 O'CLOCK, FIVE OTHER ARAB NATIONALS WERE SLATED TO BOARD AMERICAN AIRLINES FLIGHT 77, AT WASHINGTON'S DULLES AIRPORT, HEADED FOR LOS ANGELES AT 8:10...

BZZT!

HOLD IT THERE, SIR!

THREE OF THEM SET OFF AN ALARM AND WERE DIRECTED TO A SECOND METAL DETECTOR. BUT THEY QUICKLY PASSED INSPECTION.

THE SCREENER, IT WAS LATER REPORTED, SHOULD HAVE "RESOLVED" WHAT SET OFF THE ALARM.

HE DIDN'T!

NO SUCH PROBLEM WAS ENCOUNTERED BY THE FOUR ARAB NATIONALS WHO BOARDED UNITED FLIGHT 93, A BOEING 767 HEADING FOR SAN FRANCISCO FROM NEWARK INTERNATIONAL AIRPORT IN NEW JERSEY AT 8 O'CLOCK.

FLIGHT 11

7:59

AT 7:59, AMERICAN AIRLINES FLIGHT 11, PROVIDING NONSTOP SERVICE FROM BOSTON TO LOS ANGELES, TOOK OFF FROM LOGAN AIRPORT.

IT CARRIED 81 PASSENGERS AND NINE FLIGHT ATTENDANTS.

BY 8:14, FLIGHT 11 HAD ITS LAST ROUTINE COMMUNICATION WITH THE GROUND AND HAD CLIMBED TO 26,000 FEET.

THIS IS AIR TRAFFIC CONTROL. YOU CAN CLIMB TO 35,000 FEET. FLIGHT 11? FLIGHT 11? WHY DON'T YOU RESPOND?

IT NEVER RESPONDED AGA

FLIGHT 175

7:58

SCHEDULED TO DEPART AT 8:00, AT 7:58 UNITED AIRLINES FLIGHT 175 PUSHED BACK FROM ITS GATE FOR ITS DEPARTURE FROM LOGAN. THE PLANE CARRIED 56 PASSENGERS AND A CREW OF NINE.

FLIGHT 77

BUCKLE YOUR SEAT BELTS, PLEASE. WE'LL BE LEAVING IN MOMENTS.

8:10

FLIGHT 93

8:00

CALLS FROM BETTY ONG AND MADELINE SWEENEY, FLIGHT ATTENDANTS ABOARD, SAID THE HIJACKING OCCURRED AT ABOUT 8:14. TWO TERRORISTS STABBED TWO ATTENDANTS AS OTHER HIJACKERS "JAMMED THEIR WAY" INTO THE COCKPIT AND TOOK OVER THE FLIGHT. MACE WAS SPRAYED AND A BOMB THREAT WAS GIVEN TO HOLD BACK PASSENGERS.

WE'RE FINALLY OFF, LADIES AND GENTLEMEN.

UNITED 175 DID NOT TAKE OFF UNTIL 8:14...

...JUST AS AMERICAN FLIGHT 11 WAS BEING HIJACKED.

8:20

AMERICAN AIRLINES FLIGHT 77 WAS SCHEDULED TO DEPART FROM WASHINGTON'S DULLES AIRPORT FOR LOS ANGELES AT 8:10. IT CARRIED 58 PASSENGERS AND A CREW OF FOUR FLIGHT ATTENDANTS.

IT TOOK OFF AT 8:20 AND REACHED ITS CRUISING ALTITUDE OF 35,000 FEET AT 8:46.

SCHEDULED TO LEAVE NEWARK AIRPORT AT 8 O'CLOCK-- FITTING INTO THE TERRORISTS' PLAN OF FOUR FLIGHTS LEAVING AT ABOUT THE SAME TIME-- UNITED FLIGHT 93 HAD TO SIT ON THE GROUND FOR 42 MINUTES BECAUSE OF HEAVY TRAFFIC.

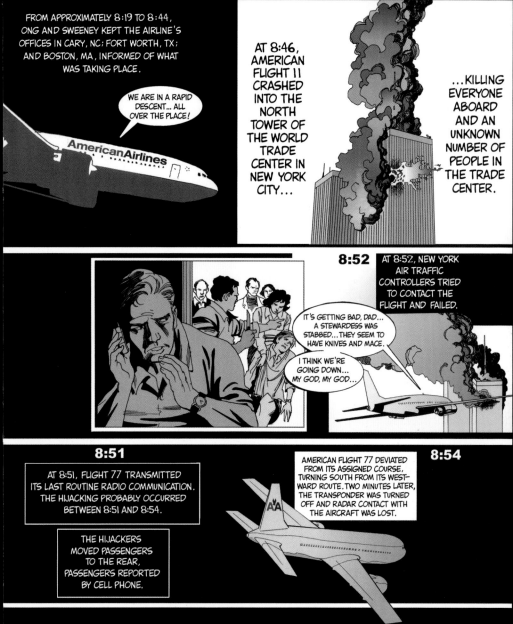

MINUTES LATER, AT 9:03, UNITED AIRLINES FLIGHT 175 STRUCK THE SOUTH TOWER...

...KILLING ALL ABOARD ALONG WITH AN UNKNOWN NUMBER OF PEOPLE IN THE TOWER.

WHOOOM!

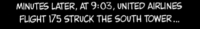

MOVE! MOVE!

THEY HAVE KNIVES AND BOX CUTTERS!

BETWEEN 9:16 AND 9:26, ON FLIGHT 77, PASSENGER BARBARA OLSON CALLED HER HUSBAND, TED OLSON, THE SOLICITOR GENERAL OF THE UNITED STATES. SHE REPORTED THAT THE FLIGHT HAD BEEN HIJACKED BY PEOPLE WHO WERE NOT AWARE OF HER CALL. SHE TOLD HIM THAT PASSENGERS WERE PUSHED TO THE BACK OF THE PLANE. THE CALL WAS CUT OFF WITHIN A MINUTE.
THE SOLICITOR GENERAL TRIED UNSUCCESSFULLY TO REACH ATTORNEY GENERAL JOHN ASHCROFT.

9:19

WHILE MAYHEM CONTINUED ON AMERICAN FLIGHT 77, FLIGHT 93'S CROSS-COUNTRY TRIP PROCEEDED ROUTINELY. UNITED DISPATCHER ED BALLINGER BEGAN TO NOTIFY AIRCRAFT TO TAKE DEFENSIVE ACTION AT 9:19.

9:23

AT 9:23, UNITED FLIGHT 93 RECEIVED ITS WARNING FROM ED BALLINGER, AND PILOT JASON DAHL RESPONDED WITH PUZZLEMENT.

ED, CONFIRM THAT LATEST MESSAGE, PLEASE-- JASON.

THE FIRES RAGED IN BOTH
TOWERS OF THE TRADE
CENTER AS FIRST
RESPONDERS WORKED
TO EVACUATE PEOPLE.

9:29

AT 9:29, FLIGHT 77, 38 MILES
WEST OF THE PENTAGON,
DISENGAGED ITS AUTOPILOT.

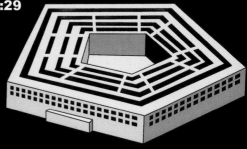

9:28

THE HIJACKERS ATTACKED
FLIGHT 93 AT 9:28 WHILE
TRAVELING 35,000
FEET ABOVE EASTERN OHIO.
THERE WERE FOUR OF THEM,
WHILE THE OTHER HIJACKED
PLANES HAD FIVE.
THE PROBABLE FIFTH WOULD—
BE HIJACKER HAD BEEN
DENIED ENTRY BY A SUSPICIOUS
IMMIGRATION OFFICIAL
IN FLORIDA.

A SECOND RADIO
TRANSMISSION 35
SECONDS LATER
INDICATED THAT A
FIGHT FOR CONTROL
OF THE AIRCRAFT
WAS STILL GOING ON.

AT 9:34, RONALD REAGAN WASHINGTON NATIONAL AIRPORT ADVISED THE SECRET SERVICE THAT AN UNKNOWN AIRCRAFT WAS HEADING IN THE DIRECTION OF THE WHITE HOUSE. BUT FIVE MILES WEST-SOUTHWEST OF THE PENTAGON, FLIGHT 77 MADE A 330-DEGREE TURN AND BEGAN DESCENDING THROUGH 2,200 FEET TOWARD THE PENTAGON AT MAXIMUM SPEED.

9:37

AT 9:37, TRAVELING ABOUT 530 MILES PER HOUR, AMERICAN FLIGHT 77 CRASHED INTO THE PENTAGON, KILLING ALL ON BOARD AS WELL AS MANY CIVILIAN AND MILITARY PERSONNEL IN THE BUILDING.

AT 9:32, ZIAD JARRAH, THE LEAD HIJACKER AND PILOT, ANNOUNCED TO THE PASSENGERS THAT THERE WAS A BOMB ON BOARD. HE THEN INSTRUCTED THE PLANE'S AUTOPILOT TO TURN THE AIRCRAFT AROUND AND HEAD EAST.

SHORTLY THEREAFTER, AT LEAST TEN PASSENGERS AND TWO CREW MEMBERS MADE CELL PHONE CALLS AND LEARNED ABOUT THE CRASHES AT THE WORLD TRADE CENTER.

9:32

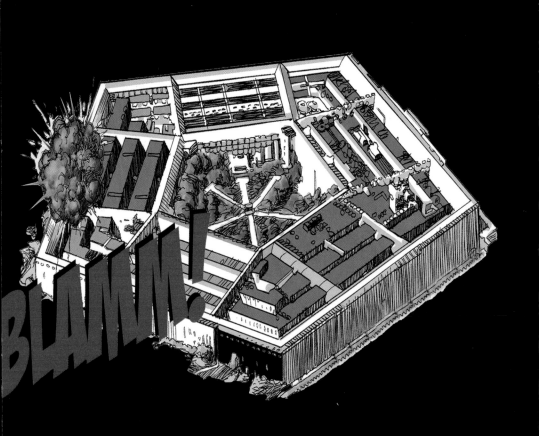

BLAMM!

9:39

AT 9:39, THE FAA'S CLEVELAND AIR ROUTE TRAFFIC CONTROL CENTER OVERHEARD A SECOND ANNOUNCE- MENT THAT THERE WAS A BOMB ABOARD AND THAT THE PLANE WAS RETURNING TO THE AIRPORT.

THAT'S NOT THE PILOT'S VOICE. SOMETHING'S GOING ON THERE.

AT 9:57, AFTER A DECISION BY THE PASSENGERS TO TAKE ACTION, THEIR ASSAULT BEGAN.

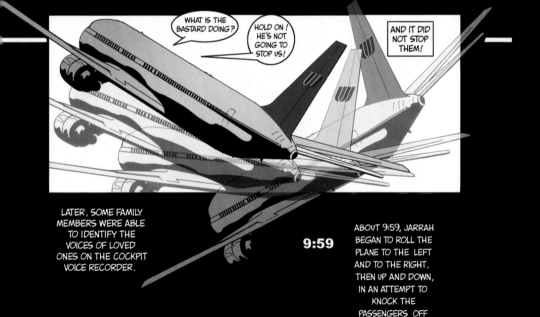

AT 10:28, THE NORTH TOWER COLLAPSED, ONE HOUR AND FORTY TWO MINUTES AFTER AMERICAN FLIGHT 11 CRASHED INTO IT.

THE NUMBER OF LIVES LOST THAT DAY WAS 2,973, THE LARGEST LOSS OF LIFE EVER ON AMERICAN SOIL AS A RESULT OF HOSTILE ATTACK.

FLIGHT 11

10:28

FLIGHT 93

10:02

AT 10:02, A HIJACKER SAID, "PULL IT DOWN," AND JARRAH DID.

THE AIRCRAFT PLOWED INTO AN EMPTY FIELD IN SHANKSVILLE, PENNSYLVANIA, ABOUT TWENTY MINUTES' FLYING TIME FROM WASHINGTON, DC, AND THE HIJACKERS' OBJECTIVE OF EITHER THE CAPITOL BUILDING OR THE WHITE HOUSE.
THEY WERE DEFEATED BY THE ALERTED THOUGH UNARMED PASSENGERS OF UNITED 93.

MAINTAINING A SAFE DISTANCE BETWEEN AIRBORNE AIRCRAFT.

THERE ARE 22 AIR TRAFFIC CONTROL CENTERS, AND A
SYSTEM COMMAND CENTER IN HERNDON, VIRGINIA.
ON 9/11, THE FOUR HIJACKED AIRCRAFT WERE
MONITORED MAINLY BY THE CENTERS IN BOSTON,
NEW YORK, CLEVELAND, AND INDIANAPOLIS.
EACH CENTER KNEW PART OF WHAT WAS GOING ON,
BUT WHAT ONE KNEW WAS NOT NECESSARILY
KNOWN BY THE OTHERS.

NORAD, A BINATIONAL COMMAND
BETWEEN THE UNITED STATES
AND CANADA, WAS ESTABLISHED IN 1958 TO
DEFEND AND, ORIGINALLY, PROTECT THE
CONTINENT AGAINST SOVIET BOMBERS.
BY THE 1990S, OTHER INTERNAL AND
EXTERNAL THREATS WERE IDENTIFIED,
BUT NORAD WAS SCALED DOWN.
BY 9/11, ITS ONETIME 26 ALERT
SITES HAD BEEN REDUCED TO 7. TWO
WERE PART OF NEADS. THE PROTOCOLS FOR
FAA AND NORAD COLLABORATION REQUIRED
MULTIPLE LEVELS OF NOTIFICATION
AND APPROVAL; THEY WERE
UNSUITED IN EVERY RESPECT FOR
WHAT HAPPENED ON 9/11.

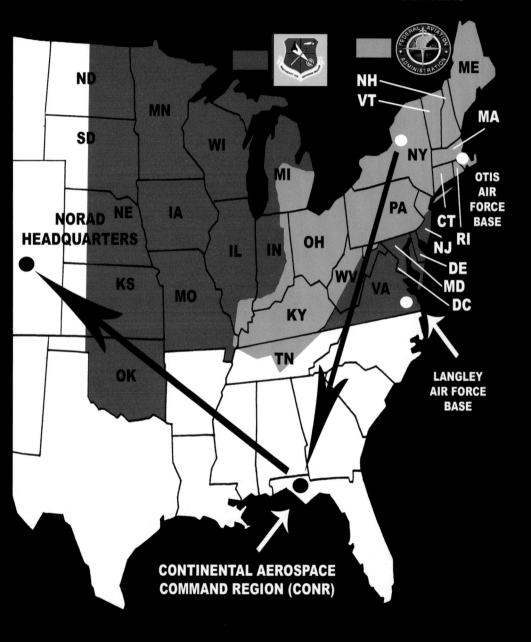

NORTHEAST AIR DEFENSE SECTOR REPORTING STRUCTURE (NEADS)

FAA TRAFFIC CONTROL CENTERS

ND

MN

SD

WI

MI

NE

IA

NORAD HEADQUARTERS

IL

IN

OH

KS

MO

KY

WV

VA

OK

TN

NH

VT

ME

MA

NY

OTIS AIR FORCE BASE

PA

CT

RI

NJ

DE

MD

DC

LANGLEY AIR FORCE BASE

CONTINENTAL AEROSPACE COMMAND REGION (CONR)

Awareness, Notification, and Response

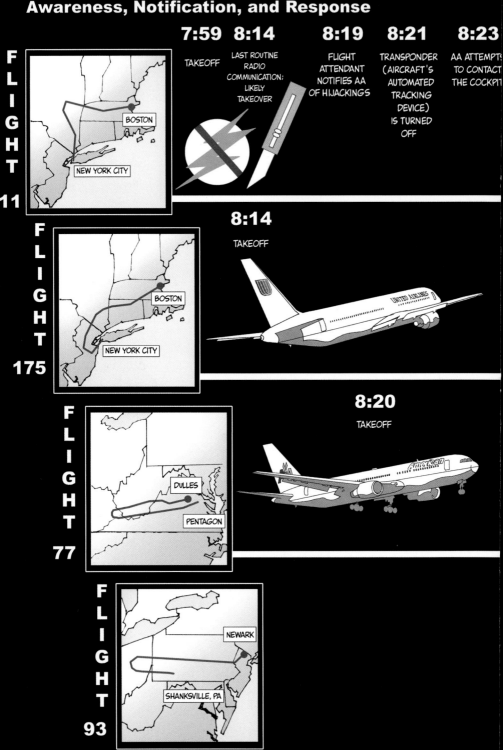

FLIGHT 11

7:59 TAKEOFF

8:14 LAST ROUTINE RADIO COMMUNICATION; LIKELY TAKEOVER

8:19 FLIGHT ATTENDANT NOTIFIES AA OF HIJACKINGS

8:21 TRANSPONDER (AIRCRAFT'S AUTOMATED TRACKING DEVICE) IS TURNED OFF

8:23 AA ATTEMPTS TO CONTACT THE COCKPIT

BOSTON

NEW YORK CITY

FLIGHT 175

8:14 TAKEOFF

BOSTON

NEW YORK CITY

FLIGHT 77

8:20 TAKEOFF

DULLES

PENTAGON

FLIGHT 93

NEWARK

SHANKSVILLE, PA

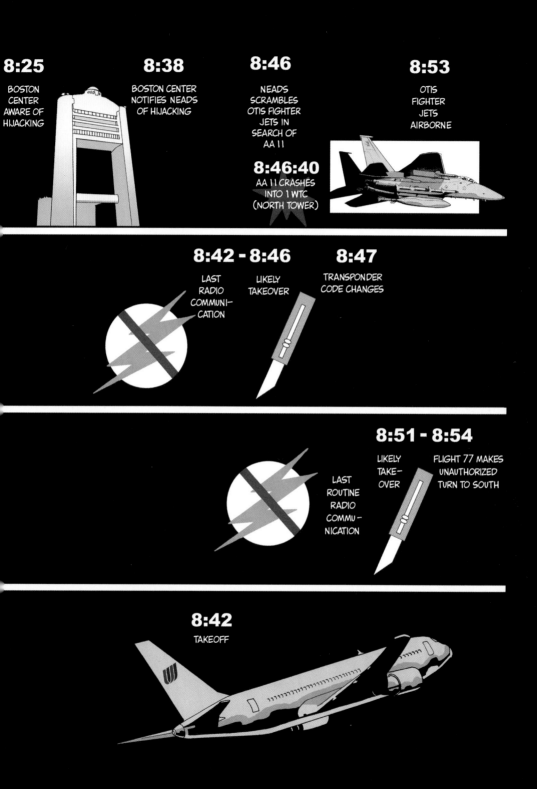

8:25
BOSTON CENTER AWARE OF HIJACKING

8:38
BOSTON CENTER NOTIFIES NEADS OF HIJACKING

8:46
NEADS SCRAMBLES OTIS FIGHTER JETS IN SEARCH OF AA 11

8:53
OTIS FIGHTER JETS AIRBORNE

8:46:40
AA 11 CRASHES INTO 1 WTC (NORTH TOWER)

8:42 - 8:46
LAST RADIO COMMUNI- CATION

LIKELY TAKEOVER

8:47
TRANSPONDER CODE CHANGES

8:51 - 8:54
LAST ROUTINE RADIO COMMU- NICATION

LIKELY TAKE- OVER

FLIGHT 77 MAKES UNAUTHORIZED TURN TO SOUTH

8:42
TAKEOFF

21

FLIGHT 11

FLIGHT 175

8:52	8:54	8:55	9:03:11
FLIGHT ATTENDANT NOTIFIES UA OF HIJACKING	UA ATTEMPTS TO CONTACT THE COCKPIT	NEW YORK CENTER SUSPECTS HIJACKING	FLIGHT 175 CRASHES INTO 2 WTC (SOUTH TOWER)

FLIGHT 77

8:56	9:05
TRANSPONDER IS TURNED OFF	AA HEAD QUARTER AWARE TH FLIGHT 7 IS HIJACK

FLIGHT

9:16
AA HEADQUARTERS AWARE THAT FLIGHT 11 HAS CRASHED INTO WTC

9:21
BOSTON CENTER ADVISES NEADS THAT AA 11 IS AIRBORNE, HEADING FOR WASHINGTON

9:24
NEADS SCRAMBLES LANGLEY FIGHTER JETS IN SEARCH OF AA 11

9:15
NEW YORK CENTER ADVISES NEADS THAT UA 175 WAS THE SECOND AIRCRAFT THAT CRASHED INTO WTC

9:20
UA HEAD—QUARTERS AWARE THAT FLIGHT 175 HAD CRASHED INTO WTC

9:25
HERNDON COMMAND CENTER ORDERS NATION—WIDE GROUND STOP

9:24
FLIGHT 93 RECEIVES WARNING FROM UA ABOUT THREAT OF POSSIBLE COCKPIT INTRUSION

FLIGHT 11

FLIGHT 175

FLIGHT 77

9:32

DULLES
TOWER
OBSERVES
RADAR OF
FAST-
MOVING
AIRCRAFT
(LATER
IDENTIFIED
AS AA 77)

9:34

FAA ADVISES
NEADS
THAT AA 77
IS MISSING

9:37:46

AA 77
CRASHES
INTO THE
PENTAGON

FLIGHT 93

9:27

LAST
ROUTINE
RADIO
COMMUNICATION

9:28

LIKELY
TAKEOVER

9:34

HERNDON
COMMAND
CENTER
ADVISES
FAA HEAD-
QUARTERS
THAT UA 93
IS HIJACKED

9:36

FLIGHT
ATTENDANT
NOTIFIES UA
OF HIJACKING;
UA ATTEMPTS
TO CONTACT
THE COCKPIT

9:41

TRAN-
SPONDER
IS TURNED
OFF

10:30

AA HEADQUARTERS CONFIRMS FLIGHT 77 CRASH INTO PENTAGON

0:03:11

FLIGHT 93 CRASHES IN FIELD IN SHANKSVILLE, PA

10:15

UA HEADQUARTERS, WASHINGTON CENTER, AND NEADS AWARE THAT FLIGHT 93 HAS CRASHED

National Crisis Management

LOOK AT THAT!

DAMN! HOW COULD THAT HAPPEN?

WHEN AMERICAN FLIGHT 11 STRUCK THE WORLD TRADE CENTER AT 8:46, NO ONE IN THE WHITE HOUSE OR TRAVELING WITH THE PRESIDENT KNEW IT HAD BEEN HIJACKED.

MOST FEDERAL AGENCIES LEARNED ABOUT THE CRASH FROM CNN.

WE'RE ON TIME, MR. PRESIDENT, FOR YOUR BOOK READING AND YOUR TALK ON EDUCATION.

IN SARASOTA, FLORIDA, THE PRESIDENTIAL MOTORCADE WAS ARRIVING AT EMMA E. BOOKER ELEMENTARY SCHOOL.

EMMA E. BOOKE[R]

THE PRESIDENT WAS OUTSIDE THE CLASSROOM WITH CHIEF OF STAFF ANDREW CARD WHEN SENIOR ADVISER KARL ROVE INFORMED THEM...

A TWIN-ENGINE PLANE HAS CRASHED INTO THE WORLD TRADE CENTER, MR. PRESIDENT.

OH, NO! MUST HAVE BEEN PILOT ERROR!

AT 8:55, BEFORE THE PRESIDENT ENTERED THE CLASSROOM, SECURITY ADVISER CONDOLEEZZA RICE SPOKE TO HIM FROM THE WHITE HOUSE.

A TWIN-ENGINE AIRCRAFT--NO, WAIT--I MEAN A COMMERCIAL AIRCRAFT.

THAT'S ALL WE KNOW RIGHT NOW, MR. PRESIDENT.

VICE PRESIDENT CHENEY HAD JUST SAT DOWN AT A WHITE HOUSE MEETING WHEN HIS ASSISTANT TOLD HIM...

TURN ON THE TELEVISION, MR. VICE PRESIDENT. A PLANE HAS STRUCK THE NORTH TOWER OF THE WORLD TRADE CENTER.

HOW THE HELL COULD A PLANE——

OH, NO! A SECOND ONE!

THE FAA, THE WHITE HOUSE, AND THE DEFENSE DEPARTMENT EACH INITIATED A MULTIAGENCY TELE-CONFERENCE BEFORE 9:30.

THE NATIONAL MILITARY COMMAND CENTER (NMCC) STARTED ITS CONFERENCE CALL AT 9:37.

DO WE HAVE EVERYONE HERE WHO SHOULD BE HERE?

I D-DON'T THINK SO.

NONE OF THESE TELECONFERENCES INCLUDED THE RIGHT OFFICIALS FROM THE FAA OR DEFENSE DEPARTMENT UNTIL 10 O'CLOCK.

27

BY 10:03, THE WHITE HOUSE CONFERENCE KNEW THAT OTHER PLANES WERE MISSING. AUTHORITY TO SHOOT DOWN AIRCRAFT WAS SOUGHT.

ALSO AT 10:03, UNITED 93 CRASHED IN PENNSYLVANIA. THE WHITE HOUSE WAS UNAWARE OF ITS HIJACKING, AND THE FAA HAD NOT YET BEEN ADDED TO THE TELECONFERENCE.

YOU MEAN WE STILL CAN'T GET HOLD OF THE RIGHT PEOPLE FROM FAA?

I CAN'T SEEM TO GET THROUGH.

AND I CAN'T LOCATE THEIR SECURE PHONE NUMBERS.

THE FAA REPRESENTATIVE WHO FINALLY JOINED THE CALL AT 10:17 HAD NO RESPONSIBILITY FOR HIJACKINGS OR ACCESS TO SENIOR DECISION MAKERS.

I'M SORRY, BUT I HAVE NONE OF THAT INFORMATION.

THAT'S THE BEST WE COULD GET?

ONE WITNESS RECALLED, "IT WAS ALMOST LIKE THERE WERE PARALLEL DECISION-MAKING PROCESSES GOING ON."

JCS VICE CHAIRMAN RICHARD MYERS DID NOT JOIN THE CONFERENCE UNTIL 10:00, AND DEFENSE SECRETARY RUMSFELD, WHO COULD NOT BE LOCATED FOR LONG PERIODS, JOINED THE CONFERENCE SHORTLY BEFORE 10:30.

THE LINES OF COMMUNICATION, FOR WHATEVER REASONS, WERE OBVIOUSLY NOT WORKING WELL.

Some of the Commission's Conclusions

THE AIRLINES FACED AN ESCALATING NUMBER OF CONFLICTING AND ERRONEOUS REPORTS OF OTHER FLIGHTS AS WELL AS A LACK OF VITAL INFORMATION FROM THE FAA ABOUT THE HIJACKED FLIGHTS.

WE FOUND NO EVIDENCE THAT AMERICAN AIRLINES SENT ANY COCKPIT WARNINGS TO ITS AIRCRAFT ON 9/11.

ALTHOUGH THE COMMAND CENTER LEARNED FLIGHT 77 WAS MISSING, NEITHER IT NOR THE FAA HEADQUARTERS ISSUED AN ALL POINTS BULLETIN TO SURROUNDING CENTERS TO SEARCH FOR PRIMARY RADAR TARGETS. AMERICAN 77 TRAVELED UNDETECTED FOR 36 MINUTES HEADING DUE EAST FOR WASHINGTON, DC.

UNITED'S FIRST DECISIVE ACTION DID NOT COME UNTIL 9:19, WHEN FLIGHT DISPATCHER ED BALLINGER BEGAN TRANSMITTING WARNINGS TO HIS SIXTEEN TRANSCONTINENTAL FLIGHTS.

WHEN AMERICAN 11 STRUCK THE WORLD TRADE CENTER AT 8:46, NO ONE IN THE WHITE HOUSE OR TRAVELING WITH THE PRESIDENT KNEW THAT IT HAD BEEN HIJACKED. WHILE THAT INFORMATION CIRCULATED WITHIN THE FAA, WE FOUND NO EVIDENCE THAT THE HIJACKING WAS REPORTED TO ANY OTHER AGENCY IN WASHINGTON BEFORE 8:46.

FAA AND **NORAD** WERE UNPREPARED FOR THE TYPE OF ATTACKS LAUNCHED AGAINST THE UNITED STATES ON SEPTEMBER 11, 2001.

BOSTON CENTER DID NOT FOLLOW PROTOCOL IN SEEKING MILITARY ASSISTANCE THROUGH THE PRESCRIBED CHAIN OF COMMAND.

AS IT TURNED OUT, THE **NEADS** AIR DEFENDERS HAD NINE MINUTES' NOTICE ON THE FIRST HIJACKED PLANE AND NO ADVANCE NOTICE ON THE SECOND, THE THIRD, OR THE FOURTH.

NOT UNTIL 9:05 DID BOSTON CENTER CONFIRM FOR BOTH **FAA** AND **NORAD** THAT HIJACKERS ABOARD AMERICAN FLIGHT 11 SAID, "WE HAVE SOME PLANES."

THE CONFLICT DID NOT BEGIN ON 9/11. IT HAD BEEN PUBLICLY DECLARED YEARS EARLIER, MOST NOTABLY IN A DECLARATION FAXED EARLY IN 1998 TO AN ARABIC-LANGUAGE NEWSPAPER IN LONDON BY THE FOLLOWERS OF A SAUDI EXILE GATHERED IN ONE OF THE MOST REMOTE AND IMPOVERISHED COUNTRIES ON EARTH.

Chapter 2:

THE FOUNDATION OF THE NEW TERRORISM

A Declaration of War

IN FEBRUARY 1998, 40-YEAR-OLD SAUDI EXILE USAMA BIN LADIN AND FUGITIVE EGYPTIAN PHYSICIAN AYMAN AL ZAWAHIRI ARRANGED FOR AN ARABIC NEWSPAPER IN LONDON TO PUBLISH A FATWA.

THEY CALLED FOR THE MURDER OF ANY AMERICAN ANYWHERE ON EARTH AS THE "INDIVIDUAL DUTY FOR EVERY MUSLIM WHO CAN DO IT IN ANY COUNTRY IN WHICH IT IS POSSIBLE TO DO IT."

THREE MONTHS LATER, BIN LADIN WAS INTERVIEWED IN AFGHANISTAN BY ABC-TV...

IT IS MORE IMPORTANT FOR MUSLIMS TO KILL AMERICANS THAN OTHER INFIDELS...

...TO KILL A SINGLE AMERICAN SOLDIER THAN TO SQUANDER EFFORTS IN OTHER ACTIVITIES.

PROMISING TO RESTORE PRIDE, DRIVE U.S. TROOPS FROM SAUDI ARABIA, AND REDRESS GRIEVANCES SUCH AS AMERICA'S SUPPORT OF ISRAEL, HE TAPPED INTO SOCIAL AND ECONOMIC MALAISE TO BUILD A FOLLOWING.

DO YOU APPROVE OF TERRORISM AND ATTACKS ON CIVILIANS? HE WAS THEN ASKED.

WE BELIEVE THAT THE WORST THIEVES IN THE WORLD TODAY AND THE WORST TERRORISTS ARE THE AMERICANS.

WE DO NOT HAVE TO DIFFERENTIATE BETWEEN MILITARY AND CIVILIAN. AS FAR AS WE ARE CONCERNED, THEY ARE ALL TARGETS.

CITING THE SOVIET ARMY'S WITHDRAWAL FROM AFGHANISTAN AS PROOF THAT A RAGGED ARMY OF DEDICATED MUSLIMS COULD OVERCOME A SUPERPOWER, HE WENT ON...

WE ARE CERTAIN THAT WE SHALL-- WITH THE GRACE OF ALLAH -- PREVAIL OVER THE AMERICANS.

AND IF THE PRESENT INJUSTICE CONTINUES... IT WILL INEVITABLY MOVE THE BATTLE TO AMERICAN SOIL.

The Rise of Bin Laden and al Qaeda

THE LARGEST NUMBERS CAME FROM THE MIDDLE EAST.

YOUNG MUSLIMS FROM AROUND THE WORLD CAME TO AFGHANISTAN TO JOIN A JIHAD, A HOLY WAR, AGAINST THE ENEMY.

...AND AMONG THEM WAS USAMA BIN LADIN.

THE 17TH OF 57 CHILDREN OF A SAUDI CONSTRUCTION MAGNATE, BIN LADIN WAS 6'5," ATHLETIC, A SKILLED HORSEMAN, RUNNER, CLIMBER, AND SOCCER PLAYER.

BUT MOST IMPORTANT, HE HAD ACCESS TO HIS FAMILY'S HUGE FORTUNE.

THROUGH HIS CONNECTIONS, BIN LADIN HELPED SET UP A FINANCIAL SUPPORT NETWORK KNOWN AS THE "GOLDEN CHAIN," WHICH INCLUDED FINANCIERS IN SAUDI ARABIA AND THE PERSIAN GULF STATES...

...WITH MONEY FLOWING THROUGH CHARITIES AND OTHER NON-GOVERNMENTAL ORGANIZATIONS.

TURKEY

TURKMENISTAN

IRAN

IRAQ

UNITED ARAB EMIRATES

KUWAIT

BAHRAIN

EGYPT

SAUDI ARABIA

QATAR

OMAN

SUDAN

YEMEN

PERSIAN GULF REGION

ETHIOPIA

SOMALIA

32

MOSQUES, SCHOOLS, AND BOARDINGHOUSES SERVED AS RECRUITING STATIONS IN MANY PARTS OF THE WORLD...

...INCLUDING THE UNITED STATES.

THEIR AGENTS ROAMED WORLD MARKETS TO BUY ARMS AND SUPPLIES FOR AFGHANISTAN'S "HOLY WARRIORS" (THE MUJAHIDEEN).

AT THIS TIME THE UNITED STATES SUPPLIED BILLIONS IN SECRET ASSISTANCE TO REBEL GROUPS FIGHTING THE SOVIETS IN AFGHANISTAN, THOUGH LITTLE OR NOTHING WAS GIVEN TO BIN LADIN.

APRIL 1988...

...BROUGHT VICTORY FOR THE AFGHAN JIHAD.

AND THE SOVIETS WERE OUT OF THE COUNTRY WITHIN NINE MONTHS.

WHEN BIN LADIN'S ACCOMPLICE, THE CLERIC ABDULLAH AZZAM, AND BOTH HIS SONS WERE KILLED IN A CAR BOMBING ON NOVEMBER 24, 1989...

...BIN LADIN WAS THE UNDISPUTED LEADER OF AL QAEDA AND **MAK** (THE ORGANIZATION CHANNELING RECRUITS INTO AFGHANISTAN).

IN AUGUST 1990, IRAQ INVADED KUWAIT AND THE CELEBRATED TERRORIST LEADER PROPOSED SUMMONING MUJAHIDEEN TO RETAKE IT.

BUT HE WAS REBUFFED BY THE SAUDI MONARCHY, WHICH INSTEAD JOINED THE AMERICANS AGAINST IRAQ. BIN LADIN DENOUNCED THEIR DECISION AND...

...HE WAS STRIPPED OF HIS SAUDI CITIZENSHIP AND HIS FUNDS WERE FROZEN. HE RELUCTANTLY STOLE AWAY TO A WELCOMING SUDAN.

HERE, IN 1991, HE SET UP A LARGE AND COMPLEX SET OF INTERTWINED BUSINESS AND TERRORIST ENTERPRISES. HE USED HIS CONSTRUCTION COMPANY TO BUILD A NEW HIGHWAY FROM KHARTOUM TO PORT SUDAN.

...AND HE USED HIS BUSINESSES TO BUY WEAPONS, EXPLOSIVES, AND TECHNICAL EQUIPMENT FOR TERRORIST PURPOSES.

HE HAD A VISION OF HIMSELF AS THE HEAD OF AN INTERNATIONAL JIHAD CON-FEDERATION, A GIGANTIC ISLAMIC ARMY OF TERRORISM THAT ENLISTED GROUPS FROM THE MIDDLE EAST, AFRICA, AND ASIA.

Nations from Which Bin Ladin Has Drawn Terrorists

THAILAND

INDONESIA

OMAN

NIGERIA

SAUDI ARABIA

LIBYA

TUNISIA

SOMALIA

UGANDA

MOROCCO

MALI

JORDAN

CHAD

BURMA

MALAYSIA

ERITREA

NIGER

ALGERIA

IRAQ

LEBANON

EGYPT

36

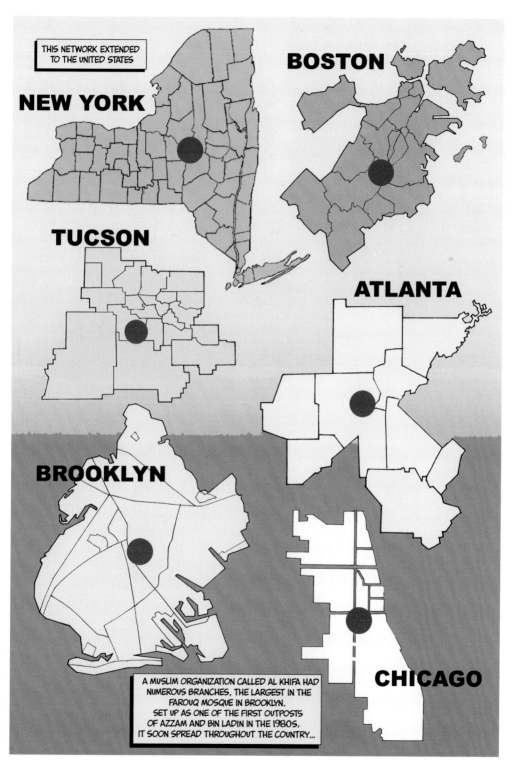

THIS NETWORK EXTENDED
TO THE UNITED STATES

NEW YORK

BOSTON

TUCSON

ATLANTA

BROOKLYN

CHICAGO

A MUSLIM ORGANIZATION CALLED AL KHIFA HAD
NUMEROUS BRANCHES, THE LARGEST IN THE
FAROUQ MOSQUE IN BROOKLYN.
SET UP AS ONE OF THE FIRST OUTPOSTS
OF AZZAM AND BIN LADIN IN THE 1980S,
IT SOON SPREAD THROUGHOUT THE COUNTRY...

37

al Qaeda's Renewal in Afghanistan (1996 - 1998)

UNDER PRESSURE FROM VARIOUS WESTERN AND ARAB STATES, SUDAN DEMANDED BIN LADIN LEAVE.

ON MAY 19, 1996, BIN LADIN-- WITH FAMILY MEMBERS, BODYGUARDS, AND AL QAEDA OFFICIALS--LEFT SUDAN ON A LEASED AIRCRAFT FOR JALALABAD, AFGHANISTAN.

AL QAEDA ENJOYED A FREEDOM OF MOVEMENT HERE IT DIDN'T HAVE IN SUDAN.

WITH PROBABLE APPROVAL BY NEIGHBORING PAKISTAN, AFGHANISTAN, NOW MOSTLY UNDER TALIBAN RULE, BECAME A WILLING NEW HAVEN.

THEY ENTERED AND EXITED WITHOUT VISAS OR IMMIGRATION PROCEDURES...

...THEY TRAVELED FREELY THROUGHOUT THE COUNTRY...

...THEY PURCHASED AND IMPORTED VEHICLES AND WEAPONS...

BLAM!

...AND THEY TRAINED AND INDOCTRINATED FROM 10,000 TO 20,000 TERRORISTS FROM 1996 TILL 9/11.

BIN LADIN HAD AGAIN BECOME THE RICH MAN OF THE JIHAD MOVEMENT. ON AUGUST 7, 1998, SIX MONTHS AFTER HIS PUBLIC FATWA AGAINST THE U.S., TEAMS IN KENYA AND TANZANIA DROVE BOMB-LADEN TRUCKS INTO THE AMERICAN EMBASSIES IN NAIROBI AND DAR ES SALAAM...

DESTROYING THE NAIROBI EMBASSY WHILE KILLING 12 AMERICANS AND 201 OTHERS, MOSTLY KENYAN, AND INJURING ABOUT 5,000 PEOPLE... ...11 MORE PEOPLE DIED IN THE ATTACK ON DAR ES SALAAM.

Chapter 3: COUNTERTERRORISM EVOLVES

From the Old Terrorism to the New

ON FEBRUARY 26, 1993, AT 18 MINUTES AFTER NOON, TERRORISTS SET OFF A HUGE TRUCK BOMB IN THE UNDERGROUND GARAGE OF THE TWIN TOWERS IN NEW YORK. THE ENSUING EXPLOSION OPENED A HOLE SEVEN STORIES HIGH, KILLING SIX PEOPLE AND INJURING THOUSANDS.

THE RELATIVELY LOW NUMBER OF FATALITIES WAS DEEMED A MIRACLE BY THE FBI. AND RAMZI YOUSEF, A CENTRAL FIGURE IN THE ATTACK, SAID LATER THAT HE HAD HOPED THE BOMB WOULD KILL 250,000.

THE FBI AND THE JUSTICE DEPARTMENT DID EXCELLENT WORK IN THEIR INVESTIGATION. WITHIN DAYS THE FBI IDENTIFIED A TRUCK REMNANT AS PART OF A RENTED VAN REPORTED STOLEN IN NEW JERSEY.

DAYS LATER, ON MARCH 4, 1993, THE FBI ARRESTED MOHAMMED SALAMEH, WHO HAD RENTED THE TRUCK AND WHO HAD KEPT CALLING THE RENTAL AGENCY TO GET BACK HIS $400 DEPOSIT.

IN SHORT ORDER, THE BUREAU HAD SEVERAL PLOTTERS IN CUSTODY. AN UNFORTUNATE CONSEQUENCE OF THIS EXCELLENT WORK WAS THAT IT CREATED THE IMPRESSION THAT THE LAW ENFORCEMENT SYSTEM WAS WELL EQUIPPED TO COMBAT TERRORISM.

AND THE TRIAL DID NOT BRING THE BIN LADIN NETWORK TO THE ATTENTION OF THE PUBLIC OR POLICY MAKERS. THE PUBLIC IMAGE WAS NOT OF THE CLEVER RAMZI YOUSEF, WHO HAD DEVISED THE BOMB AND WOULD NOT BE CAPTURED UNTIL 1995, BUT OF STUPID SALAMEH, GOING BACK AGAIN AND AGAIN TO RECLAIM HIS $400 DEPOSIT.

Adaptation--and Nonadaptation--in the Law Enforcement Community

THEIR SO-CALLED CLUBROOM WAS LOADED WITH HORSE.

DESPITE THE WORLD TRADE CENTER BOMBING IN 1993, NOT VERY MUCH WAS ADDED TO OUR COUNTER-TERRORISM DEFENSES.

AGENTS CONTINUED TO WORK ON TRADITIONAL CRIMES...

...SUCH AS WHITE-COLLAR OFFENSES AND THOSE PERTAINING TO DRUGS AND GANGS.

IN THE FBI'S 56 FIELD OFFICES, BECAUSE OF ITS LENGTHY INVESTIGATIONS AND LOW NUMBER OF ARRESTS, COUNTERTERRORISM WAS NOT CONSIDERED CAREER ENHANCING.

COUNTERTERRORISM UNIT

THE FBI IN 1998, UNDER DIRECTOR LOUIS FREEH, ISSUED A FIVE-YEAR PLAN THAT DESIGNATED NATIONAL SECURITY, INCLUDING COUNTERTERRORISM, A TOP PRIORITY.

IT DID NOT SUCCEED.

THEY TRIPLED OUR BUDGET, BUT LEFT US UNDERSTAFFED.

IN THE YEAR 2000, THERE WERE STILL TWICE AS MANY AGENTS DEVOTED TO DRUG ENFORCEMENT AS TO COUNTERTERRORISM.

DIDN'T WE FINALLY HIRE AN AGENT WHO UNDERSTOOD ARABIC?

I CAN'T MAKE HEADS OR TAILS OF THIS.

BETTER PUT THIS REPORT AWAY--HE'S FROM JUSTICE.

A MISUNDERSTANDING OF JUSTICE DEPARTMENT RULES CREATED AN ATTITUDE CALLED "THE WALL" THAT HINDERED THE SHARING OF INFORMATION BETWEEN THE FBI AND THE JUSTICE DEPARTMENT'S CRIMINAL DIVISION.

THIS PREVENTED INFORMATION LEARNED FROM THE NATIONAL SECURITY AGENCY AND THE CIA FROM BEING SHARED WITH CRIMINAL INVESTIGATORS.

CONTINUING THE TRADITION OF HIRING ANALYSTS FROM WITHIN, THE FBI DID NOT HAVE AGENTS WITH THE RELEVANT EDUCATIONAL BACKGROUND.

LET THEM THROUGH. THEIR NAMES AREN'T ON THE LIST.

FRANKLY, I CAN'T EVEN READ THEIR NAMES.

THOUGH THE IMMIGRATION AND NATURALIZATION SERVICE (INS) HAD PERHAPS THE GREATEST POTENTIAL TO DEVELOP AN EXPANDED ROLE IN COUNTERTERRORISM, IT HAD OUTDATED TECHNOLOGY, USED MANUAL TYPEWRITERS, WAS STILL USING PAPER WATCH LISTS, AND DID NOT EFFECTIVELY DETER FRAUDULENT APPLICANTS. IN FACT, INSPECTORS AT THE PORTS OF ENTRY WERE NOT ASKED TO FOCUS ON TERRORISTS.

...and in the Federal Aviation Administration

PRIOR TO 9/11, THE FAA SET AND ENFORCED AVIATION AND SECURITY RULES THAT AIRLINES AND AIRPORTS WERE REQUIRED TO IMPLEMENT.

THE RESULTING "LAYERED DEFENSE" OF INTELLIGENCE PRESCREENING, CHECKPOINT SCREENING, AND ONBOARD SECURITY WAS SERIOUSLY FLAWED...

...AND FAILED TO STOP ANY OF THE 9/11 HIJACKERS FROM BOARDING ON THAT FATEFUL DAY.

DO I SEND THIS TO THE FAA?

NO NEED.

THE FAA NO-FLY LIST CONTAINED JUST 12 TERRORIST SUSPECTS, THOUGH THE GOVERNMENT WATCH LISTS CONTAINED MANY THOUSANDS.

YOU'RE ALL RIGHT. GO AHEAD.

THE WEAKNESSES WERE MANY...

IMPORTANT INFORMATION ABOUT POTENTIAL TERRORIST ACTIVITY WAS NOT PASSED TO FAA HEADQUARTERS.

METAL DETECTORS AND X-RAY MACHINES PERFORMED POORLY AND OFTEN FAILED TO DETECT PROHIBITED ITEMS.

I'M SCHEDULED FOR THE FLIGHT TO LONDON. AND YOU?

TO LISBON AND ON TO TOKYO.

THE FAA'S FOCUS WAS ON OPERATIONAL CONCERNS AND SAFETY. NOT ON TERRORISM!

FEDERAL AVIATION ADMINISTRATION

AS OF 9/11, THERE WERE ONLY 33 ARMED AND TRAINED AIR MARSHALS, AND NONE WERE DEPLOYED ON U.S. DOMESTIC FLIGHTS.

...and in the Intelligence Community

DCI: THE DIRECTOR OF CENTRAL INTELLIGENCE HEADS THE U.S. INTELLIGENCE COMMUNITY.
CREATED IN 1947, CENTRAL INTELLIGENCE (CIA) IS AN INDEPENDENT AGENCY THAT COLLECTS, ANALYZES, AND DISSEMINATES INTELLIGENCE FROM ALL SOURCES. ITS POWER OVER THE CONFEDERATED "INTELLIGENCE COMMUNITY," HOWEVER, IS LIMITED. THE DIRECTOR REPORTS DIRECTLY TO THE PRESIDENT.

NATIONAL SECURITY AGENCY (NSA), PART OF THE DEFENSE DEPARTMENT, INTERCEPTS AND ANALYZES FOREIGN COMMUNICATIONS AND BREAKS CODES. IT ALSO CREATES CODES AND CIPHERS TO PROTECT GOVERNMENT INFORMATION. (DEFENSE DEPARTMENT AGENCIES ACCOUNT FOR 80% OF UNITED STATES SPENDING ON INTELLIGENCE.)

NATIONAL RECONNAISSANCE OFFICE DEVELOPS, PROCURES, LAUNCHES, AND MAINTAINS IN ORBIT INFORMATION- GATHERING SATELLITES THAT SERVE OTHER GOVERNMENT AGENCIES. ALSO PART OF THE DEFENSE DEPARTMENT.

NATIONAL GEOSPATIAL-INTELLIGENCE AGENCY (NGA), ALSO PART OF THE DEFENSE DEPARTMENT, PROVIDES AND ANALYZES A WIDE ARRAY OF PRODUCTS, INCLUDING MAPS, NAVIGATION TOOLS, AND SURVEILLANCE INTELLIGENCE.

THE DEFENSE INTELLIGENCE AGENCY SUPPORTS THE SECRETARY OF DEFENSE, JOINT CHIEFS OF STAFF, AND MILITARY FIELD COMMANDERS.

THE ARMY, NAVY, AIR FORCE, AND MARINE CORPS HAVE THEIR OWN INTELLIGENCE COMPONENTS THAT COLLECT INFORMATION, HELP THEM DECIDE WHAT WEAPONS TO ACQUIRE, AND SERVE THE TACTICAL NEEDS OF THEIR RESPECTIVE SERVICES.

BESIDES THESE, THE FBI, THE STATE DEPARTMENT, THE TREASURY DEPARTMENT, THE ENERGY DEPARTMENT, THE COAST GUARD, AND NOW THE DEPARTMENT OF HOMELAND SECURITY EACH HAS ITS OWN SECURITY PARTS.

THE CIA IS A DESCENDANT OF THE OFFICE OF STRATEGIC SERVICES (OSS), CREATED IN 1942 BY PRESIDENT FRANKLIN DELANO ROOSEVELT DURING WORLD WAR II...

I HAD HOPED THE FBI WOULD OFFER US OUR NEEDED STRATEGIC SERVICES IN EUROPE, BILL...

BUT NOW I'M LEAVING IT UP TO YOU TO ESTABLISH THAT FORCE!

AND ARMY COLONEL WILLIAM J. (WILD BILL) DONOVAN, A FAMED WALL STREET LAWYER, DEVELOPED AND LED THAT SUCCESSFUL DEPARTMENT, THE COUNTRY'S FIRST SPY NETWORK.

TO DONOVAN'S DISAPPOINTMENT, PRESIDENT HARRY S. TRUMAN DISSOLVED THE OSS AT THE END OF THE WAR.

I'M SORRY, BILL. THE WAR IS OVER AND SO IS THIS DEPARTMENT.

BUT FOUR MONTHS LATER, THE COLD WAR MADE IT NECESSARY TO CREATE THE CENTRAL INTELLIGENCE GROUP HEADED BY A DIRECTOR OF INTELLIGENCE.

THIS SEPARATION OF POWER BUILT IN TENSION BETWEEN THE CIA AND DEFENSE DEPARTMENT AS WELL AS THE CIA AND THE FBI.

MR. PRESIDENT, YOU CAN'T GIVE ONE AGENCY ALL THAT POWER. THAT COULD CREATE A GESTAPO!

YOU BELIEVE THE FBI IS FIT TO RUN INTERNAL SECURITY, MR. HOOVER?

THE COLD WAR'S END LEFT THE CIA WEAKENED (ONLY 25 NEW OFFICERS JOINED IN 1995) BY BUDGET CUTS, SECURITY CONCERNS, AND SATELLITES REPLACING COVERT ACTIONS.

CREATED TO WAGE THE COLD WAR, THE CIA INVESTMENTS IN RESEARCH COULD NOT HELP OTHER PROBLEMS.

THE CIA FAILED TO FORESEE THE NUCLEAR TESTS BY INDIA AND PAKISTAN IN 1998.

IT FAILED IN ITS WARNING SYSTEMS AGAINST TERRORISM.

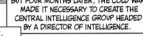

IT HAD LIMITED ABILITY TO ASSESS THE BALLISTIC MISSILE THREAT TO THE UNITED STATES.

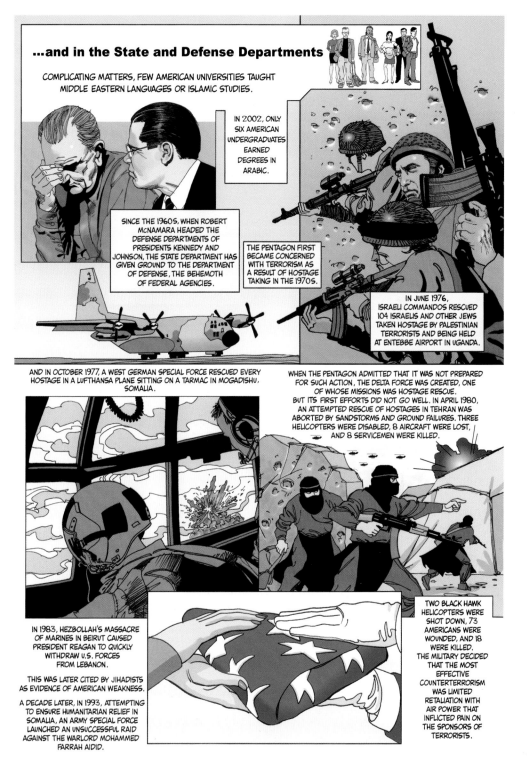

...and in the State and Defense Departments

COMPLICATING MATTERS, FEW AMERICAN UNIVERSITIES TAUGHT MIDDLE EASTERN LANGUAGES OR ISLAMIC STUDIES.

IN 2002, ONLY SIX AMERICAN UNDERGRADUATES EARNED DEGREES IN ARABIC.

SINCE THE 1960S, WHEN ROBERT McNAMARA HEADED THE DEFENSE DEPARTMENTS OF PRESIDENTS KENNEDY AND JOHNSON, THE STATE DEPARTMENT HAS GIVEN GROUND TO THE DEPARTMENT OF DEFENSE, THE BEHEMOTH OF FEDERAL AGENCIES.

THE PENTAGON FIRST BECAME CONCERNED WITH TERRORISM AS A RESULT OF HOSTAGE TAKING IN THE 1970S.

IN JUNE 1976, ISRAELI COMMANDOS RESCUED 104 ISRAELIS AND OTHER JEWS TAKEN HOSTAGE BY PALESTINIAN TERRORISTS AND BEING HELD AT ENTEBBE AIRPORT IN UGANDA.

AND IN OCTOBER 1977, A WEST GERMAN SPECIAL FORCE RESCUED EVERY HOSTAGE IN A LUFTHANSA PLANE SITTING ON A TARMAC IN MOGADISHU, SOMALIA.

WHEN THE PENTAGON ADMITTED THAT IT WAS NOT PREPARED FOR SUCH ACTION, THE DELTA FORCE WAS CREATED, ONE OF WHOSE MISSIONS WAS HOSTAGE RESCUE. BUT ITS FIRST EFFORTS DID NOT GO WELL. IN APRIL 1980, AN ATTEMPTED RESCUE OF HOSTAGES IN TEHRAN WAS ABORTED BY SANDSTORMS AND GROUND FAILURES. THREE HELICOPTERS WERE DISABLED, 8 AIRCRAFT WERE LOST, AND 8 SERVICEMEN WERE KILLED.

IN 1983, HEZBOLLAH'S MASSACRE OF MARINES IN BEIRUT CAUSED PRESIDENT REAGAN TO QUICKLY WITHDRAW U.S. FORCES FROM LEBANON.

THIS WAS LATER CITED BY JIHADISTS AS EVIDENCE OF AMERICAN WEAKNESS.

A DECADE LATER, IN 1993, ATTEMPTING TO ENSURE HUMANITARIAN RELIEF IN SOMALIA, AN ARMY SPECIAL FORCE LAUNCHED AN UNSUCCESSFUL RAID AGAINST THE WARLORD MOHAMMED FARRAH AIDID.

TWO BLACK HAWK HELICOPTERS WERE SHOT DOWN, 73 AMERICANS WERE WOUNDED, AND 18 WERE KILLED. THE MILITARY DECIDED THAT THE MOST EFFECTIVE COUNTERTERRORISM WAS LIMITED RETALIATION WITH AIR POWER THAT INFLICTED PAIN ON THE SPONSORS OF TERRORISTS.

Some of the Commission's Conclusions:

THE IRAN—CONTRA SCANDAL AT THE END OF THE REAGAN ADMINISTRATION—— SECRETLY TRADING HOSTAGES FOR ARMS AND DIVERTING THE PROCEEDS TO ANTI—COMMUNIST GUERRILLAS—— CAST A CLOUD OVER THE NOTION THAT THE WHITE HOUSE SHOULD DIRECT COUNTERTERRORISM.

HOWEVER, AFTER THE WORLD TRADE CENTER BOMBING IN 1993 AND THE IRAQI ATTEMPT TO KILL THE FIRST PRESIDENT BUSH, THE CLINTON ADMINISTRATION TURNED TO VETERAN CIVIL SERVANT RICHARD CLARKE TO DEVELOP THE MIDLEVEL INTERAGENCY COMMITTEE EVENTUALLY TITLED THE COUNTERTERRORISM SECURITY GROUP (CSG).

CLARKE WOULD SOON BECOME MANAGER OF THE U.S. COUNTERTERRORISM EFFORT, WITH A SEAT ON THE CABINET—LEVEL PRINCIPALS COMMITTEE WHEN IT MET ON HIS ISSUES.

TERRORISM CAME UNDER THE JURISDICTION OF AT LEAST 14 DIFFERENT COMMITTEES IN THE HOUSE ALONE... AND BUDGET AND OVERSIGHT FUNCTIONS IN THE HOUSE AND SENATE CONCERNING TERRORISM WERE ALSO SPLINTERED AMONG COMMITTEES.

THE GROWING THREAT AND CAPABILITIES OF BIN LADIN WERE NOT UNDERSTOOD IN CONGRESS.

LITTLE EFFORT IN THE LEGISLATIVE BRANCH WAS MADE TO CONSIDER AN INTEGRATED POLICY TOWARD TERRORISM. ALL COMMITTEES FOUND THEMSELVES SWAMPED IN THE MINUTIAE OF THE BUDGET PROCESS, WITH LITTLE TIME FOR THE CONSIDERATION OF LONGER—TERM QUESTIONS.

EACH OF THESE TRENDS CONTRIBUTED TO WHAT CAN ONLY BE DESCRIBED AS CONGRESS' SLOWNESS AND INADEQUACY IN TREATING THE ISSUE OF TERRORISM IN THE YEARS BEFORE 9/11. THE LEGISLATIVE BRANCH ADJUSTED LITTLE AND DID NOT RESTRUCTURE ITSELF TO ADDRESS CHANGING THREATS.

Before the Bombings in Kenya and Tanzania

WE'VE SEEN A STREAM OF REPORTS ABOUT THE MAN AND HIS FINANCING OF TERRORISM...

...AS WELL AS HIS LEADERSHIP OF AN ORGANIZATION CALLED AL QAEDA.

IN 1996, THE CIA SET UP A SPECIAL UNIT OF A DOZEN OFFICERS TO ANALYZE INTELLIGENCE AND PLAN OPERATIONS AGAINST BIN LADIN.

IN MAY OF THAT YEAR, BIN LADIN LEFT HIS HAVEN IN SUDAN FOR A NEW ONE IN AFGHANISTAN.

SEVERAL MONTHS LATER, A MAN NAMED JAMAL AHMED AL FADL WALKED INTO A U.S. EMBASSY IN AFRICA AND...

I HAVE MUCH INFORMATION ON THE WORKINGS OF A SECRET ORGANIZATION CALLED AL QAEDA.

THE MAN'S DISCLOSURES WERE CORROBORATED BY SEVERAL SOURCES.

BY 1997, THE BIN LADIN SPECIAL UNIT RECOGNIZED THAT BIN LADIN WASN'T SIMPLY A FINANCIER...

HIS GROUP HAS A MILITARY COMMITTEE THAT IS PLANNING OPERATIONS AGAINST U.S. INTERESTS WORLDWIDE... AS WELL AS ATTEMPTING TO OBTAIN NUCLEAR MATERIALS.

Crisis: August 1998

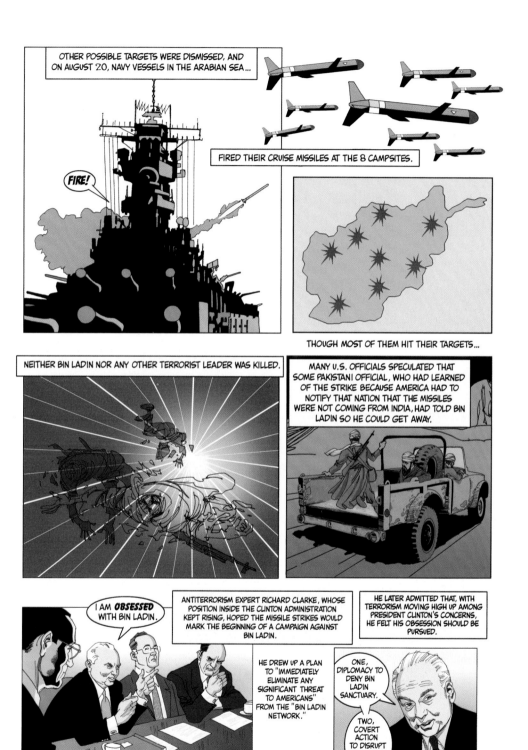

OTHER POSSIBLE TARGETS WERE DISMISSED, AND ON AUGUST 20, NAVY VESSELS IN THE ARABIAN SEA...

FIRE!

FIRED THEIR CRUISE MISSILES AT THE 8 CAMPSITES.

THOUGH MOST OF THEM HIT THEIR TARGETS...

NEITHER BIN LADIN NOR ANY OTHER TERRORIST LEADER WAS KILLED.

MANY U.S. OFFICIALS SPECULATED THAT SOME PAKISTANI OFFICIAL, WHO HAD LEARNED OF THE STRIKE BECAUSE AMERICA HAD TO NOTIFY THAT NATION THAT THE MISSILES WERE NOT COMING FROM INDIA, HAD TOLD BIN LADIN SO HE COULD GET AWAY.

I AM *OBSESSED* WITH BIN LADIN.

ANTITERRORISM EXPERT RICHARD CLARKE, WHOSE POSITION INSIDE THE CLINTON ADMINISTRATION KEPT RISING, HOPED THE MISSILE STRIKES WOULD MARK THE BEGINNING OF A CAMPAIGN AGAINST BIN LADIN.

HE LATER ADMITTED THAT, WITH TERRORISM MOVING HIGH UP AMONG PRESIDENT CLINTON'S CONCERNS, HE FELT HIS OBSESSION SHOULD BE PURSUED.

HE DREW UP A PLAN TO "IMMEDIATELY ELIMINATE ANY SIGNIFICANT THREAT TO AMERICANS" FROM THE "BIN LADIN NETWORK."

ONE, DIPLOMACY TO DENY BIN LADIN SANCTUARY.

TWO, COVERT ACTION TO DISRUPT TERRORIST ACTIVITIES.

HE ENVISIONED AN ONGOING CAMPAIGN AGAINST BIN LADIN'S BASES THAT MIGHT PERSUADE THE TALIBAN TO HAND THE MAN OVER.

THREE, CAPTURE BIN LADIN AND HIS DEPUTIES AND BRING THEM TO TRIAL.

FOUR, DRY UP BIN LADIN'S MONEY SUPPLY.

FIVE, AND PREPARE TO FOLLOW UP WITH MILITARY ACTION.

THEY'RE LITTLE BUT JUNGLE GYM CAMPS!

NOT WORTHY OF THE USE OF EXPENSIVE MISSILES.

AND THERE COULD BE LOTS OF BLOWBACK AGAINST A BOMB-HAPPY UNITED STATES.

AND WE DID NOTHING!

Diplomacy

IN 1998 AND 1999, MANY ATTEMPTS TO USE DIPLOMACY TO GET BIN LADIN FROM THE TALIBAN FAILED. AS UNDERSECRETARY OF STATE THOMAS PICKERING SAID, THEY HAD "BORNE LITTLE FRUIT." SO THE CLINTON ADMINISTRATION TURNED TO...

Covert Action

AS PART OF THE RESPONSE TO THE EMBASSY BOMBINGS IN KENYA AND TANZANIA, THE PRESIDENT SIGNED A MEMORANDUM OF NOTIFICATION.

THIS ALLOWS THE CIA TO LET OUR TRIBAL ASSETS USE FORCE TO CAPTURE BIN LADIN AND HIS ASSOCIATES.

AND THIS IS AN EXECUTIVE ORDER TO FREEZE HIS FINANCIAL HOLDINGS.

WORKING WITH ALBANIAN AUTHORITIES, CIA OPERATIVES RAIDED AN AL QAEDA FORGERY OPERATION AND A TERRORIST CELL IN THE ALBANIAN CITY OF TIRANA...

WE'LL TAKE THOSE PAPERS *NOW!*

THESE OPERATIONS MAY HAVE DISRUPTED A PLANNED ATTACK ON THE U.S. EMBASSY IN TIRANA.

THERE WERE ARRESTS OF TERRORISTS IN AZERBAIJAN, ITALY, AND BRITAIN. OPERATIVES PREVENTED AN ATTACK ON THE U.S. EMBASSY IN UGANDA. ABU HAJER, ONE OF BIN LADIN'S TOP DEPUTIES, WAS ARRESTED IN GERMANY.

ACCORDING TO RICHARD CLARKE, AUGUST AND SEPTEMBER HAD BROUGHT "THE GREATEST NUMBER OF TERRORIST ARRESTS IN A SHORT PERIOD OF TIME THAT WE HAVE EVER FACILITATED."

ON OCTOBER 26, RICHARD CLARKE'S SMALL GROUP TOOK THE UNUSUAL STEP OF HOLDING A MEETING DEDICATED TO TRYING "TO EVALUATE THE THREAT OF A TERRORIST ATTACK IN THE UNITED STATES BY THE USAMA BIN LADIN NETWORK."

YOU ARE URGED TO BE AS CREATIVE AS POSSIBLE IN YOUR THINKING ABOUT THIS.

AT TIMES THERE WERE NEW DISCUSSIONS ABOUT MISSILE ATTACKS AGAINST BIN LADIN.

KANDAHAR

WE BELIEVE BIN LADIN WILL BE IN THE GOVERNOR'S RESIDENCE IN KANDAHAR TONIGHT.

WE CAN HIT HIM TONIGHT. WE MAY NEVER GET ANOTHER CHANCE.

BUT ONCE AGAIN, QUESTIONS AROSE.

GENERAL ZINNI SAYS THERE MAY BE OVER 200 PEOPLE WHO COULD BE KILLED OR WOUNDED AND DAMAGE DONE TO A NEARBY MOSQUE.

WE BELIEVE THERE'D BE HALF AS MUCH COLLATERAL DAMAGE AND NO DANGER TO THE MOSQUE.

AND FOR ONE REASON OR ANOTHER, NO ACTION WAS TAKEN.

THOUGH IT WAS BELIEVED THAT PRESIDENT CLINTON WANTED BIN LADIN DEAD, SIMILAR KINDS OF QUESTIONS STOPPED PLANS OF USING AFGHAN TRIBALS OR AMERICAN FORCES TO ASSASSINATE HIM.

IF BIN LADIN GETS WORD OF THIS HE MAY FIND ASYLUM IN IRAQ.

WE'D NEED PAKISTANI APPROVAL TO FLY MISSILES OVER THEIR NATION.

FORGET IT! SOMEONE IN THEIR INTELLIGENCE WOULD CERTAINLY GET WORD TO BIN LADIN.

Searching for Fresh Options

DOUBTS ABOUT DIFFERENT METHODS OF RESPONSE TO AL QAEDA CONTINUED AS GENERALS AND HIGH OFFICIALS COULD NOT AGREE ON A SINGLE COURSE.

"BIN LADIN COULD MOVE TO A CITY AND A MISSILE COULD KILL THOUSANDS."

SO ONCE AGAIN, NO ACTION WAS TAKEN.

"INTELLIGENCE ISN'T GOOD ENOUGH TO FIND HIM WITH AN AC-130 GUNSHIP."

"IF WE PUT BOOTS ON THE GROUND, AND INTELLIGENCE IS FAULTY, WE'D HAVE LOSS OF LIVES IN A FRUITLESS EFFORT."

WE THOUGHT WE HAD HIM, BUT NOW WE DON'T KNOW.

750

EVERY OFFICIAL THE COMMISSION QUESTIONED ABOUT THE POSSIBILITY OF INVADING AFGHANISTAN SAID...

...IT WAS ALMOST UNTHINKABLE ABSENT A PROVOCATION SUCH AS 9/11; PROSPECTS FOR COOPERATION FROM OTHER NATIONS WERE POOR, AND THE AMERICAN PUBLIC WOULDN'T HAVE SUPPORTED IT.

CRUISE MISSILES REMAINED THE ONLY MILITARY OPTION ON THE TABLE.

IN EARLY 1999, THE CIA LEARNED THAT BIN LADIN WAS SPENDING MUCH TIME NEAR SHEIKH ALI, A DESERT HUNTING CAMP BEING USED BY VISITORS FROM THE UNITED ARAB EMIRATES.

THEY'RE GONE.

ONE WEEK LATER RICHARD CLARKE CALLED AN EMIRATI OFFICIAL TO EXPRESS HIS CONCERNS ABOUT POSSIBLE ASSOCIATIONS BETWEEN EMIRATIS AND BIN LADIN.

AND ANOTHER CHANCE TO GET THE TERRORIST WAS LOST.

SEEKING NEW PARTNERS, AMERICA TURNED TO AHMED SHAH MASSOUD, CHARISMATIC LEADER OF THE ANTI-TALIBAN FORCE, THE NORTHERN ALLIANCE.

TAJIK

THE ALLIANCE, DOMINATED BY TAJIKS, DREW ITS STRENGTH FROM THE NORTHERN AND EASTERN PARTS OF AFGHANISTAN.

THE TALIBAN MEMBERS CAME MAINLY FROM THE COUNTRY'S LARGEST ETHNIC GROUP, THE PASHTUNS, WHO ARE CONCENTRATED IN THE SOUTHERN AREAS.

PASHTUN

MASSOUD WAS AFGHANISTAN'S MOST RENOWNED MILITARY COMMANDER, BUT HIS BANDS WERE CHARGED WITH MASSACRES...

...AND HEROIN TRAFFIC.

AND STILL NO DIRECT ATTEMPT WAS MADE TO KILL BIN LADIN.

IN FEBRUARY 1999, CIA HEAD GEORGE TENET RECEIVED CLINTON'S AUTHORIZATION TO ENLIST MASSOUD IN TRACKING DOWN BIN LADIN.

TO CAPTURE HIM, NOT TO KILL HIM!

HIS BODY LANGUAGE WAS TRANSLATED AS:"YOU GUYS ARE CRAZY!"

IN THE FALL OF 1999, THE NEW CIA PLAN WAS UNVEILED.

TRYING TO PENETRATE AL QAEDA'S RANKS, INCREASE CONTACTS WITH THE NORTHERN ALLIANCE.

CONTINUED DISRUPTION, HIRING OFFICERS WITH BETTER ANTITERRORISM SKILLS...

NO OPTION WAS RATED AS HAVING OVER A 15% CHANCE OF SUCCESS.

Chapter 5: AL QAEDA AIMS AT THE AMERICAN HOMELAND

Terrorist Entrepreneurs

BY EARLY 1999, AL QAEDA WAS A POTENT ADVERSARY OF THE UNITED STATES. BIN LADIN AND HIS CHIEF OF OPERATIONS, ABU HAFS AL MASRI, WERE ITS UNDISPUTED LEADERS.
TO UNDERSTAND HOW THE ORGANIZATION WORKED AND TO INTRODUCE THE ORIGINS OF THE 9/11 PLOT, WE EXAMINE THREE OF THEIR SUBORDINATES.

1. THE PRINCIPAL ARCHITECT OF THE ATTACK WAS KHALID SHEIKH MOHAMMED (KSM).

GROWING UP IN KUWAIT, HE TRACES HIS ETHNIC LINEAGE TO THE BALUCHISTAN REGION, STRADDLING IRAN AND PAKISTAN. HE JOINED THE MUSLIM BROTHERHOOD AT 16 AND BECAME ENAMORED OF VIOLENT JIHAD AT YOUTH CAMPS IN THE DESERT.

HE TRAVELED THROUGHOUT MANY ISLAMIC REGIONS AND EARNED A DEGREE IN MECHANICAL ENGINEERING FROM A UNIVERSITY IN GREENSBORO, NORTH CAROLINA.

HE APPLIED HIS SKILLS TO AN EXTRAORDINARY ARRAY OF TERRORIST SCHEMES...

...CONVENTIONAL CAR BOMBING... POLITICAL ASSASSINATION... HIJACKING... AND, ULTIMATELY, USING AIRCRAFT AS MISSILES.

HE HAD NUMEROUS CONVERSATIONS WITH HIS NEPHEW, RAMZI YOUSEF, PRIOR TO YOUSEF'S MASTERMINDING THE TRADE CENTER BOMBING IN 1993.

...AND IN LATE 1998 OR EARLY 1999 GOT THE GREEN LIGHT AND FUNDING FOR THE 9/11 PLOT.

HE MET WITH BIN LADIN IN MID-1996, INTRODUCING HIM TO THE PLAN OF TRAINING PILOTS TO CRASH INTO U.S. BUILDINGS...

2. RIDUAN ISAMUDDIN (BETTER KNOWN AS HAMBALI) WAS BORN AND EDUCATED IN INDONESIA, AND BECAME A FOLLOWER OF EXTREMIST ISLAMIST TEACHING OF VARIOUS CLERICS, ESPECIALLY ABDULLAH SUNGKAR, IN MALAYSIA IN THE 1980S.

SENT TO AFGHANISTAN BY SUNGKAR, HE FOUGHT AGAINST THE SOVIETS IN 1986. IN 1998, HE ASSUMED RESPONSIBILITY FOR THE MALAYSIA/SINGAPORE REGION WITHIN THE CLERIC'S TERRORIST ORGANIZATION, JEMAAH ISLAMIAH, THE JI.

BY 1998, THE JI BEGAN JOINT OPERATIONS WITH AL QAEDA, MARRYING AL QAEDA'S FINANCIAL AND TECHNICAL STRENGTHS WITH JI'S ACCESS TO MATERIALS AND LOCAL OPERATIVES.

3. ABD AL RAHIM AL NASHIRI, THE MASTERMIND OF THE USS COLE BOMBING AND EVENTUAL AL QAEDA HEAD IN THE ARABIAN PENINSULA, WAS RECRUITED BY BIN LADIN HIMSELF.

WHILE ENTICING NASHIRI'S LARGE GROUP TO JOIN HIM IN A JIHAD AGAINST THE AMERICANS, BIN LADIN ENCOURAGED NASHIRI TO CASE THE PORT OF ADEN TO FIND U.S. NAVAL SHIPS TO ATTACK.

ONE RESULT WAS THE SUCCESSFUL ATTACK IN OCTOBER 2000 ON THE USS COLE.

NASHIRI'S CAPTURE IN THE UNITED ARAB EMIRATES IN NOVEMBER 2002 FINALLY ENDED HIS CAREER AS A TERRORIST.

The "Planes Operation"

ACCORDING TO KHALID SHEIKH MOHAMMED, HE STARTED TO THINK ABOUT ATTACKING THE U.S. AFTER THE TRADE CENTER BOMBING IN 1993.

HE AND HIS NEPHEW YOUSEF BRAINSTORMED AND DECIDED THAT NEW YORK CITY, THE COUNTRY'S ECONOMIC CAPITAL, WAS THE PRIME TARGET.

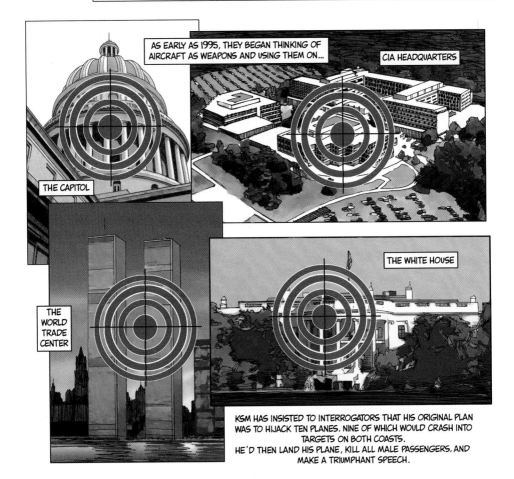

AS EARLY AS 1995, THEY BEGAN THINKING OF AIRCRAFT AS WEAPONS AND USING THEM ON...

CIA HEADQUARTERS

THE CAPITOL

THE WHITE HOUSE

THE WORLD TRADE CENTER

KSM HAS INSISTED TO INTERROGATORS THAT HIS ORIGINAL PLAN WAS TO HIJACK TEN PLANES, NINE OF WHICH WOULD CRASH INTO TARGETS ON BOTH COASTS.
HE'D THEN LAND HIS PLANE, KILL ALL MALE PASSENGERS, AND MAKE A TRIUMPHANT SPEECH.

KSM FORMALLY JOINED AL QAEDA IN LATE 1998 OR 1999 WHEN BIN LADIN DECIDED TO SUPPORT HIS PROPOSAL OF ATTACKING THE UNITED STATES WITH COMMERCIAL AIRPLANES AS WEAPONS.

IN SPRING 1999, AN INITIAL LIST OF TARGETS WAS SELECTED THAT INCLUDED THE WHITE HOUSE, THE U.S. CAPITOL, THE PENTAGON, AND THE WORLD TRADE CENTER. FOUR SUICIDE OPERATIVES WERE SELECTED: KHALID AL MIHDHAR, NAWAF AL HAZMI, KHALLAD, AND ABU BARA AL YEMENI.

THE "PLANES OPERATION" HAD BECOME REALITY.

WHEN KHALLAD APPLIED FOR A U.S. VISA, HIS APPLICATION WAS DENIED. IT WAS DECIDED THAT HE AND ABU BARA, BOTH YEMENIS, WOULD NOT RECEIVE VISAS AS EASILY AS THE OTHER TWO, WHO WERE SAUDIS.

THEY WERE SCRAPPED FROM THE ORIGINAL PLAN AND BECAME PART OF A PLOT TO HIJACK U.S. COMMERCIAL PLANES FLYING INTERNATIONAL ROUTES...

...THAT WERE TO BE EITHER DESTROYED MIDAIR OR CRASHED INTO TARGETS IN ASIA.

IN AFGHANISTAN AND THEN IN KARACHI, PAKISTAN, THE RECRUITS WERE TRAINED IN ...

...FITNESS, COMBAT, SHOOTING, NIGHT OPERATIONS, AIRLINE TIMETABLES, THE INTERNET, AND BASIC ENGLISH WORDS.

TRAINEES TRAVELED THROUGH MUCH OF EAST ASIA, TESTING WHAT CAN BE TAKEN ABOARD A PLANE, PROCEDURES IN A PLANE'S OPERATION, AND GAINING PASSPORT STAMPS TO GIVE THE APPEARANCE OF SIMPLE TOURISTS.

ON JANUARY 15, 2000, HAZMI AND MIHDHAR, THE FIRST TWO OF THE CONSPIRATORS, ARRIVED IN LOS ANGELES.

AND SEVERAL MONTHS LATER, BIN LADIN CANCELED THE EAST ASIA PART OF THE PLANES OPERATION, EVIDENTLY FEELING IT WAS TOO DIFFICULT TO COORDINATE WITH THE AMERICAN PLOT.

The Hamburg Contingent

THOUGH THE PRINCIPALS THOUGHT OF USING ESTABLISHED AL QAEDA MEMBERS FOR THE PLANES OPERATION, FOUR ASPIRING JIHADISTS ARRIVED IN KANDAHAR FROM GERMANY IN LATE 1999 AND CHANGED THEIR PLANS.

MOHAMED ATTA, RAMZI BINALSHIBH, MARWAN AL SHEHHI, AND ZIAD JARRAH ALL BECAME KEY PLAYERS IN THE 9/11 CONSPIRACY.

BINALSHIBH

JARRAH

SHEHHI

THE HAMBURG GROUP SHARED THE ANTI–U.S. FERVOR OF THE OTHERS BUT ADDED THE ENORMOUS ADVANTAGE OF FLUENCY IN ENGLISH AND FAMILIARITY WITH LIFE IN THE WEST.
LIFE THERE HAD LEFT THEM MORE, NOT LESS, RADICAL.

THERE IS A JEWISH WORLD CONSPIRACY CENTERED IN NEW YORK CITY.

YOU NOTICE THEY SPEAK ONLY IN ARABIC AND KEEP TO THEMSELVES.

ATTA

THE FOURSOME BECAME CORE MEMBERS OF A GROUP OF RADICAL MUSLIMS IN HAMBURG AFTER HOSTING SESSIONS AT THEIR APARTMENT––SOMETIMES THREE OR FOUR TIMES A WEEK––THAT INVOLVED EXTREMELY ANTI–AMERICAN DISCUSSIONS.

BY LATE 1999, THEY WERE READY TO ABANDON THEIR STUDENT LIVES IN FAVOR OF VIOLENT JIHAD.

EVIDENCE INDICATES THAT THE FOUR DECIDED TO FIGHT IN CHECHNYA AGAINST THE RUSSIANS.

ON A TRAIN IN GERMANY, THEY WERE APPROACHED (BECAUSE THEY WERE ARABS WEARING BEARDS, ONE BELIEVED) AND REFERRED TO AN AL QAEDA OPERATIVE, WHO TOLD THEM IT WAS DIFFICULT TO GET INTO CHECHNYA JUST THEN.

THEY WERE TOLD BY THE OPERATIVE TO GET PAKISTANI VISAS.
HE WOULD THEN INSTRUCT THEM ON HOW TO GET INTO AFGHANISTAN AND TO TRAIN FOR JIHAD BEFORE TRAVELING ON TO CHECHNYA.

THE SPEED WITH WHICH THE FOUR BECAME MEMBERS OF THE 9/11 PLOT, WITH ATTA DESIGNATED AS OPERATIONAL LEADER, IS REMARKABLE.

THE NEW RECRUITS POSSESSED AN IDEAL COMBINATION OF TECHNICAL SKILLS AND KNOWLEDGE THAT THE ORIGINAL OPERATIVES LACKED.

IN EARLY 2000, THEY RETURNED TO HAMBURG AND QUICKLY MADE EFFORTS TO AVOID APPEARING RADICAL.

THEY DISTANCED THEMSELVES FROM CONSPICUOUS EXTREMISTS, CUT THEIR BEARDS, NO LONGER ATTENDED MOSQUES, AND WORE WESTERN-STYLE CLOTHES.

BECAUSE FLIGHT SCHOOLS IN THE U.S. WERE LESS EXPENSIVE AND REQUIRED SHORTER TRAINING PERIODS, ATTA E-MAILED 31 DIFFERENT SUCH SCHOOLS ON BEHALF OF A SMALL GROUP OF ARABS IN GERMANY.

ATTA, SHEHHI, AND JARRAH, CLAIMING THEIR OLD ONES HAD BEEN LOST, OBTAINED NEW PASSPORTS. PRESUMABLY, THEY FEARED THAT THE PAKISTANI VISAS IN THEIR OLD PASSPORTS WOULD RAISE SUSPICIONS. BINALSHIBH, THE ONLY YEMENI IN THE GROUP, COULD NOT OBTAIN A VISA AND HAD TO BE LEFT BEHIND.

A MONEY TRAIL

BIN LADIN AND HIS AIDES DID NOT NEED A VERY LARGE SUM TO FINANCE THEIR PLANNED ATTACK IN AMERICA. THE 9/11 PLOTTERS SPENT SOMEWHERE BETWEEN $400,000 AND $500,000.

THE CIA ESTIMATES THAT IT COST AL QAEDA ABOUT $30 MILLION PER YEAR TO SUSTAIN ACTIVITIES BEFORE 9/11 AND THIS MONEY WAS RAISED ALMOST ENTIRELY THROUGH DONATIONS.

THOUGH BIN LADIN WAS ONCE THOUGHT TO HAVE AN ENORMOUS FORTUNE, THE U.S. GOVERNMENT DISCOVERED IN EARLY 2000 THAT FROM 1970 TO 1994, BIN LADIN RECEIVED ABOUT $1 MILLION PER YEAR.

THE TALIBAN SUPPORTED HIM UNTIL HE REINVIGORATED HIS FUND-RAISING EFFORTS BY DRAWING ON TIES TO WEALTHY SAUDI INDIVIDUALS DURING THE AFGHAN WAR IN 1980. THE COMMISSION FOUND NO EVIDENCE THAT THE SAUDI GOVERNMENT OR SENIOR SAUDI OFFICIALS FUNDED THE ORGANIZATION.

Chapter 6: FROM THREAT TO THREAT

The Millennium Crisis

AFTER THE BOMBINGS OF U.S. EMBASSIES IN AUGUST 1998, PRESIDENT BILL CLINTON AND HIS AIDES EXPLORED WAYS OF GETTING BIN LADIN EXPELLED FROM AFGHANISTAN.

...IF NOT EXPELLED, POSSIBLY CAPTURE HIM OR HAVE HIM KILLED.

THOUGH CONCERNED ABOUT BIN LADIN AND TERRORISM, THE PRESIDENT DELIBERATELY WOULDN'T MENTION HIS NAME.

BECAUSE, YOU SAY, YOU CHOSE NOT TO GIVE HIM UNNECESSARY PUBLICITY.

ON NOVEMBER 30, 1999, DAYS FROM THE START OF THE NEW MILLENNIUM, JORDANIAN INTELLIGENCE INTERCEPTED A PHONE CALL FROM ABU ZUBAYDAH, AN ALLY OF BIN LADIN, AND PALESTINIAN EXTREMIST KHADR ABU HOSHAR.

THE TIME FOR TRAINING IS *OVER!*

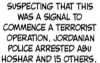

SUSPECTING THAT THIS WAS A SIGNAL TO COMMENCE A TERRORIST OPERATION, JORDANIAN POLICE ARRESTED ABU HOSHAR AND 15 OTHERS.

INFORM WASHINGTON OF WHAT WE'VE DONE.

ABU HOSHAR AND RAED HIJAZI, ONE OF THOSE ARRESTED, HAD SETTLED ON A PLAN TO HIT FOUR TARGETS IN JORDAN: THE SAS RADISSON HOTEL IN DOWNTOWN AMMAN, THE BORDER CROSSING TO ISRAEL, AND TWO CHRISTIAN HOLY SITES.

GOOD. THEY'LL ALL BE MOBBED WITH AMERICAN TOURISTS.

AND THIS WOULD BE ONLY THE BEGINNING.

ONCE HOSHAR AND HIJAZI WERE CAUGHT, JORDAN POLICE FOUND THEIR RENTED HOUSE AND DISCOVERED...

...DRUMS OF ACIDS, DETONATORS, FORGED SAUDI PASSPORTS.

AND THIS CD-ROM OF A TERRORIST MANUAL.

ON DECEMBER 4, AS NEWS CAME IN TO THE CIA ABOUT THE DISCOVERIES IN JORDAN, COUNTER-TERRORISM COORDINATOR RICHARD CLARKE WROTE NATIONAL SECURITY ADVISER SANDY BERGER...

If George's story about a planned series of UBL attacks at the Millennium is true, we will need to make some decisions NOW.

THE COMMISSION WAS TOLD THAT CLARKE HAD SEVERAL CONVERSATIONS WITH CLINTON SUGGESTING REPRISALS AGAINST THE TALIBAN IN THE EVENT OF ANY ATTACKS ON U.S. INTERESTS, ANYWHERE, BY BIN LADIN.

GENERAL PERVEZ MUSHARRAF WAS URGED TO "TAKE WHATEVER ACTION YOU DEEM NECESSARY TO RESOLVE THE BIN LADIN PROBLEM." BUT IT WAS REPORTED THAT THE PAKISTANI LEADER WAS "UNWILLING TO TAKE THE POLITICAL HEAT AT HOME."

DISRUPTION AND ARREST OPERATIONS WERE MOUNTED AGAINST TERRORISTS IN EIGHT COUNTRIES.

IN MID-DECEMBER, PRESIDENT CLINTON SIGNED A MEMORANDUM OF NOTIFICATION GIVING THE CIA BROADER AUTHORITY TO USE FOREIGN PROXIES TO DETAIN BIN LADIN LIEUTENANTS.

THEN ON DECEMBER 14, 1999, AHMED RESSAM, AN ALGERIAN JIHADIST INTENDING TO SET OFF EXPLOSIVES IN LOS ANGELES LAX AIRPORT ON OR AROUND JANUARY 1, 2000, WAS STOPPED BY CUSTOMS AGENTS AFTER FERRYING ACROSS THE CANADIAN BORDER TO PORT ANGELES, WASHINGTON, AND PLACED UNDER ARREST.

ANOTHER MILLENNIUM PLOT HAD BEEN STOPPED.

Post-Crisis Reflection
Agenda 2000

ON MARCH 10, 2000, THE PRINCIPALS COMMITTEE AGREED THE GOVERNMENT NEEDED TO TAKE THREE MAJOR STEPS.

1. MORE MONEY TO GO TO THE CIA TO "SERIOUSLY ATTRIT" AL QAEDA.

2. CRACK DOWN ON FOREIGN TERRORIST ORGANIZATIONS IN THE UNITED STATES.

3. IMMIGRATION LAW ENFORCEMENT SHOULD BE STRENGTHENED AND THERE SHOULD BE TIGHTENED CONTROLS ON THE CANADIAN BORDER.

DIRECT PRESSURE ON THE TALIBAN HAVING FAILED TO LEAD TO BIN LADIN'S CAPTURE, AMERICAN OFFICIALS MET WITH GENERAL MUSHARRAF TO WIN PAKISTAN'S INFLUENCE.

I WILL MEET WITH MULLAH OMAR AND PRESS HIM ON BIN LADIN.

BUT THE AMERICANS THOUGHT PAKISTAN WOULD NOT DO ANYTHING "GIVEN WHAT IT SEES AS THE BENEFITS OF TALIBAN CONTROL OF AFGHANISTAN."

ON MARCH 25, 2000, THE PRESIDENT MET WITH MUSHARRAF IN PAKISTAN, THE FIRST TIME A PRESIDENT HAD BEEN THERE SINCE 1969.

"I OFFERED HIM THE MOON IN TERMS OF BETTER RELATIONS," SAID CLINTON, "IF HE'D HELP US GET BIN LADIN."

NEITHER THAT NOR VISITS FROM OTHERS SWAYED THE PAKISTANI LEADER TO ACTION. BY SEPTEMBER, THE U.S. WAS OPENLY CRITICAL...

THE PAKISTANI GOVERNMENT CONTINUES TO SUPPORT A TALIBAN MILITARY OFFENSIVE AIMED AT THE CONQUEST OF AFGHANISTAN.

AK-47
AK-47
AK-47

THE TALIBAN DID NOT EXPEL BIN LADIN, AND PAKISTANI ARMS CONTINUED TO FLOW ACROSS THE BORDER.

WHOOOSH!

FLAM!

AS SECRETARY OF STATE MADELINE ALBRIGHT TOLD THE COMMISSION: "WE DID NOT HAVE A STRONG HAND TO PLAY WITH THE PAKISTANIS."

INTERNAL DISPUTES AND UNDERFUNDING HAMPERED RICHARD CLARKE'S AND THE PRINCIPAL COMMITTEE'S 3-POINT AGENDA DURING THE FOLLOWING MONTHS. BUT THEN CAME...

The Attack on the USS <u>Cole</u>

ON OCTOBER 12, 2000, AL QAEDA OPERATIVES IN A SMALL BOAT LADEN WITH EXPLOSIVES APPROACHED THE USS <u>COLE</u> IN THE PORT OF ADEN.

AS THE BOAT CAME ALONGSIDE THE AMERICAN DESTROYER, THE AL QAEDA OPERATIVES MADE FRIENDLY GESTURES TO THE CREW.

BUT SECONDS LATER...

BLAM!

WE NOW KNOW THAT THIS WAS A FULL-FLEDGED AL QAEDA OPERATION SUPERVISED DIRECTLY BY BIN LADIN.

KILLING 17 MEMBERS OF THE CREW AND WOUNDING AT LEAST 40.

EXPECTING AMERICAN RETALIATION, BIN LADIN HAD AL QAEDA'S KANDAHAR AIRPORT COMPOUND EVACUATED AND THEN FLED FROM ONE HIDEAWAY TO ANOTHER.

THERE WAS NO AMERICAN STRIKE, AND BIN LADIN DECIDED TO LAUNCH SOMETHING BIGGER.

TEAMS FROM THE FBI, THE NAVAL CRIMINAL INVESTIGATIVE SERVICE (NCIS), AND THE CIA WERE IMMEDIATELY SENT TO YEMEN TO INVESTIGATE THE ATTACK. WITHIN A FEW WEEKS THE OUTLINE OF THE STORY BEGAN TO EMERGE.

SAUDI ARABIA

YEMEN

ADEN

THIS LIST OF SUSPECTS INCLUDES THE AL QAEDA AFFILIATE, EGYPTIAN ISLAMIC JIHAD.

TO PROVE IT WAS BIN LADIN WE NEED MORE!

WE NEED A LINK TO SOMEONE KNOWN AS AN AL QAEDA OPERATIVE.

WITHIN WEEKS AFTER THE ATTACK, THE YEMENIS ARRESTED AND INTERROGATED BADAWI AND QUSO, TWO IMPORTANT SUSPECTS, WHO NAMED KHALLAD (TAWFIQ BIN ATTASH), BIN LADIN'S "RUN BOY" WHO HAD HELPED DIRECT THE ATTACK FROM AFGHANISTAN OR PAKISTAN.

THOUGH U.S. INTELLIGENCE AGENCIES HAD CONNECTED KHALLAD TO OTHER AL QAEDA TERRORIST OPERATIONS, PRESIDENT CLINTON TOLD THE COMMISSION THAT BEFORE HE COULD TAKE FURTHER ACTION...

...THE CIA AND FBI HAD TO "BE WILLING TO STAND UP IN PUBLIC AND SAY WE BELIEVE BIN LADIN DID THIS."

BUSH SWORN IN, CLINTON LEAVES OFFICE

RICHARD CLARKE AND HIS STAFF PREPARED A POLICY PAPER OF THEIR OWN:
* ROLL BACK AL QAEDA OVER A PERIOD OF 3-5 YEARS.
* COVERT AID TO THE NORTHERN ALLIANCE AND UZBEKISTAN AND RENEWED PREDATOR FLIGHTS IN MARCH 2001.
* MILITARY ACTION TO DESTROY AL QAEDA COMMAND-AND-CONTROL TARGETS AND INFRASTRUCTURE, TALIBAN MILITARY AND COMMAND ASSETS.
* CONCERN ABOUT THE PRESENCE OF AL QAEDA OPERATIVES IN THE U.S.

THE PRESIDENT SAID THAT HE WAS VERY FRUSTRATED THAT HE COULD NOT GET A DEFINITIVE ENOUGH ANSWER TO DO SOMETHING ABOUT THE COLE ATTACK. NO SUCH ANSWER WAS GIVEN BEFORE HIS ADMINISTRATION LEFT OFFICE.

THE ELECTION OF NOVEMBER 7, 2000--ONE OF THE CLOSEST CONTESTS IN U.S. HISTORY--BROUGHT IN A NEW ADMINISTRATION HEADED BY TEXAS GOVERNOR GEORGE W. BUSH AS PRESIDENT. MEMORIES DIFFER AS TO WHAT WAS AND WASN'T SAID DURING THE TRANSITION.

Change and Continuity

I THINK YOU'LL FIND THAT, BY FAR, YOUR BIGGEST THREAT IS BIN LADIN AND THE AL QAEDA.

ONE OF THE GREAT REGRETS OF MY PRESIDENCY IS THAT I DIDN'T GET HIM [BIN LADIN] FOR YOU, BECAUSE I TRIED TO.

PRESIDENT GEORGE W. BUSH SAID HE FELT SURE PRESIDENT CLINTON MENTIONED TERRORISM, BUT HE DID NOT REMEMBER MUCH BEING SAID ABOUT AL QAEDA.

SAMUEL "SANDY" BERGER, CLINTON'S NATIONAL SECURITY ADVISER, SAID THAT HE TOLD RICE THAT THE BUSH ADMINISTRATION SHOULD SPEND MORE TIME ON TERRORISM IN GENERAL AND AL QAEDA IN PARTICULAR THAN ON ANYTHING ELSE.

CONDOLEEZZA RICE, BUSH'S NATIONAL SECURITY ADVISER, RECALLED THAT BERGER TOLD HER SHE WOULD BE SURPRISED AT HOW MUCH MORE TIME SHE WAS GOING TO SPEND ON TERRORISM THAN SHE EXPECTED, BUT THE BULK OF THEIR CONVERSATION DEALT WITH THE MIDDLE EAST AND NORTH KOREA.

RICE DECIDED TO KEEP CLARKE, BUT HE WOULD NOW REPORT TO DEPUTIES, NOT DIRECTLY TO THE PRINCIPALS COMMITTEE. THE DECISION TO KEEP CLARKE WAS "NOT UNCONTROVERSIAL" SINCE HE WAS KNOWN AS SOMEONE WHO "BROKE CHINA."

RICHARD CLARKE, NATIONAL COUNTERTERRORISM COORDINATOR, WAS DISAPPOINTED AT WHAT HE PERCEIVED AS A DEMOTION.

WE *URGENTLY* NEED A PRINCIPALS LEVEL REVIEW ON THE AL QAEDA NETWORK.

I HOPE THAT WE CAN GATHER ENOUGH INTELLIGENCE TO FIGURE OUT WHO DID THE ACT [THE COLE ATTACK] AND TAKE THE NECESSARY ACTION. THERE MUST BE A CONSEQUENCE.

CLARKE APPROACHED RICE IN AN EFFORT TO GET HER-- AND THE NEW PRESIDENT-- TO GIVE TERRORISM A VERY HIGH PRIORITY AND TO ACT ON THE AGENDA THAT HE HAD PUSHED DURING THE LAST FEW MONTHS OF THE PREVIOUS ADMINISTRATION.

I'M TIRED OF PLAYING DEFENSE. I WANT TO PLAY OFFENSE. I WANT TO TAKE THE FIGHT TO THE TERRORISTS.

CLARKE SAID DECISIONS SHOULD BE MADE ON "WHEN AND HOW TO RESPOND TO THE ATTACK ON THE USS COLE."

The New Administration's Approach

DISCUSSIONS BETWEEN GOVERNMENT DEPARTMENTS AND BETWEEN INDIVIDUALS ENDED WITH LITTLE OR NO CHANGE IN POLICY. AS HOPE OF PERSUADING THE TALIBAN TO TURN OVER BIN LADIN FADED, COVERT ACTION TO TOPPLE ITS LEADERSHIP WAS DISCUSSED.

RICHARD CLARKE AND THE CIA'S COFER BLACK RENEWED THE PUSH TO AID THE NORTHERN ALLIANCE, BUT THIS, AGAIN, WENT UNRESOLVED.

COMMANDER OF CENTRAL COMMAND GENERAL TOMMY FRANKS TOLD THE COMMISSION THAT HE DID NOT REGARD THE EXISTING PLANS TO ADDRESS AL QAEDA AS SERIOUS.

AT THE JOINT CHIEFS OF STAFF, GENERAL HUGH SHELTON DID NOT RECALL MUCH INTEREST BY THE NEW ADMINISTRATION IN MILITARY OPERATIONS AGAINST AL QAEDA IN AFGHANISTAN.

RICHARD CLARKE, HOWEVER, REMAINED CONSISTENT. IN A MEMO TO NATIONAL SECURITY ADVISER CONDOLEEZZA RICE, HE WROTE...

"DECISION MAKERS SHOULD IMAGINE THEMSELVES ON A FUTURE DAY WHEN THE CSG HAS NOT SUCCEEDED IN STOPPING AL QAEDA ATTACKS AND HUNDREDS OF AMERICANS LAY DEAD IN SEVERAL COUNTRIES, INCLUDING THE U.S."

ON SEPTEMBER 9, TWO DAYS BEFORE THE ATTACK BY TERRORISTS IN THE U.S., AHMED SHAH MASSOUD, THE LEADER OF THE NORTHERN ALLIANCE, WAS KILLED IN A BOMB PLOT BY TWO AL QAEDA ASSASSINS DISGUISED AS JOURNALISTS.

Chapter 7: THE ATTACK LOOMS

First Arrivals in California

ON JANUARY 15, 2000, NAWAF AL HAZMI AND KHALID AL MIHDHAR, TWO OF THE TERRORISTS ON FLIGHT 77, ARRIVED IN LOS ANGELES AND SPENT TWO WEEKS THERE BEFORE MOVING ON TO SAN DIEGO.

YOU ARE STILL NOT SAYING IT CORRECTLY, MR. HAZMI.

THEY WERE DIRECTED TO ENROLL IN ENGLISH CLASSES SO THEY COULD LEARN THE LANGUAGE AND BEGIN PILOT TRAINING.

KHALID SHEIKH MOHAMMED, ORGANIZER OF THE PLANES OPERATION, DENIES THERE WERE AL QAEDA AGENTS IN CALIFORNIA. THE COMMISSION DOES NOT CREDIT THIS DENIAL. THEY BELIEVE IT UNLIKELY THAT THE TWO, NEITHER OF WHOM SPOKE ENGLISH, WOULD COME TO THE U.S. WITHOUT ASSISTANCE AWAITING THEM.

THEY APPEARED TO HAVE OBTAINED ASSISTANCE FROM THE MUSLIM COMMUNITY, SPECIFICALLY THE ONE SURROUNDING THE PROMINENT KING FAHD MOSQUE IN CULVER CITY.

BY FEBRUARY, THE TWO MOVED TO SAN DIEGO, POSSIBLY DRIVEN THERE BY MOHDAR ABDULLAH, A YEMENI UNIVERSITY STUDENT.

ABDULLAH TOLD THE FBI THAT HE KNEW OF THE MEN'S EXTREMIST VIEWS AND MIHDHAR'S INVOLVEMENT WITH THE ISLAMIC ARMY OF ADEN, WHICH HAD AL QAEDA TIES.

ABDULLAH DENIED ADVANCE KNOWLEDGE OF THE ATTACK, BUT IN PRISON AS A MATERIAL WITNESS AFTER 9/11, HE TOLD OTHER INMATES...

I HEARD ABOUT THEIR PLANS IN SAN DIEGO.

THEY TOLD ME THEY PLANNED TO FLY AN AIRPLANE INTO A BUILDING.

THE FBI HAS NOT BEEN ABLE TO VERIFY HIS STATEMENTS.

IN SAN DIEGO, THE TWO MEN RENTED A ROOM OWNED BY AN INDIVIDUAL THEY MET AT A MOSQUE.

HAZMI AND MIHDHAR MIXED IN WELL WITH THE CITY'S ISLAMIC COMMUNITY. ABDULLAH HELPED THEM GET DRIVER'S LICENSES AND APPLY TO LANGUAGE AND FLIGHT SCHOOLS.

NEW LICENSES

THE COMMISSION'S IMPRESSION IS THAT HAZMI AND MIHDHAR SOUGHT AND FOUND A GROUP OF LIKE—MINDED MUSLIMS WITH ROOTS IN YEMEN AND SAUDI ARABIA ASSOCIATED WITH MOHDAR ABDULLAH AND THE RABAT MOSQUE IN LA MESA.

HAZMI AND MIHDHAR CAME TO THE U.S. TO LEARN ENGLISH, TAKE FLYING LESSONS, AND BECOME PILOTS.

STRUGGLING TO ADAPT AND HOMESICK, MIHDHAR MOVED BACK TO YEMEN ON JUNE 10, 2000. HAZMI STAYED ON AND WAS JOINED BY HANI HANJOUR, THE NEWLY ARRIVED HIJACKER PILOT.

FLIGHT SIMULATOR

THEY SOON LEARNED THEY WERE CAPABLE OF NEITHER.

HANJOUR HAD ARRIVED IN SAN DIEGO ON DECEMBER 8, AND DAYS LATER HE AND HAZMI DISAPPEARED...

CAFE

WALK

733.41.

...SUPPOSEDLY TO TAKE FLYING LESSONS IN SAN JOSE.

The 9/11 Pilots in the United States

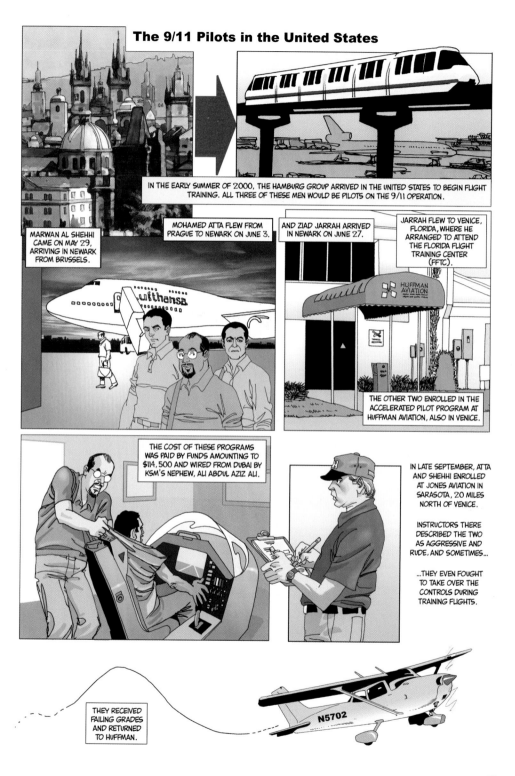

IN THE EARLY SUMMER OF 2000, THE HAMBURG GROUP ARRIVED IN THE UNITED STATES TO BEGIN FLIGHT TRAINING. ALL THREE OF THESE MEN WOULD BE PILOTS ON THE 9/11 OPERATION.

MOHAMED ATTA FLEW FROM PRAGUE TO NEWARK ON JUNE 3.

MARWAN AL SHEHHI CAME ON MAY 29, ARRIVING IN NEWARK FROM BRUSSELS.

AND ZIAD JARRAH ARRIVED IN NEWARK ON JUNE 27.

JARRAH FLEW TO VENICE, FLORIDA, WHERE HE ARRANGED TO ATTEND THE FLORIDA FLIGHT TRAINING CENTER (FFTC).

THE OTHER TWO ENROLLED IN THE ACCELERATED PILOT PROGRAM AT HUFFMAN AVIATION, ALSO IN VENICE.

THE COST OF THESE PROGRAMS WAS PAID BY FUNDS AMOUNTING TO $114,500 AND WIRED FROM DUBAI BY KSM'S NEPHEW, ALI ABDUL AZIZ ALI.

IN LATE SEPTEMBER, ATTA AND SHEHHI ENROLLED AT JONES AVIATION IN SARASOTA, 20 MILES NORTH OF VENICE.

INSTRUCTORS THERE DESCRIBED THE TWO AS AGGRESSIVE AND RUDE, AND SOMETIMES...

...THEY EVEN FOUGHT TO TAKE OVER THE CONTROLS DURING TRAINING FLIGHTS.

THEY RECEIVED FAILING GRADES AND RETURNED TO HUFFMAN.

N5702

IN EARLY AUGUST, JARRAH OBTAINED A SINGLE–ENGINE PRIVATE PILOT CERTIFICATE. HE PROMPTLY FLEW TO GERMANY TO SPEND TIME WITH HIS GIRLFRIEND, AYSEL SENGUEN, THE FIRST OF FIVE FOREIGN TRIPS HE TOOK DURING THIS PERIOD.

RAMZI BINALSHIBH, WHO WAS SUPPOSED TO BE AT FFTC WITH JARRAH, FAILED TO OBTAIN A U.S. VISA IN FOUR ATTEMPTS.

VISA REJECTED

UNABLE TO BECOME THE FOURTH PILOT IN THE ATTACK, HE TOOK THE ROLE OF COORDINATING BETWEEN KSM AND THE OPERATIVES IN THE U.S.

HANI HANJOUR, WHO ALREADY HAD HIS PRIVATE PILOT'S LICENSE AND AN FAA–ISSUED COMMERCIAL PILOT CERTIFICATE, BECAME THAT FOURTH PILOT.

HANJOUR HAD SPENT MUCH TIME IN ARIZONA PREVIOUSLY. HE HAD ASSOCIATED WITH SEVERAL INDIVIDUALS HOLDING EXTREMIST BELIEFS WHO HAVE BEEN THE SUBJECT OF COUNTERTERRORISM INVESTIGATIONS.

HE WAS IN MESA, ARIZONA, AT THIS TIME, WITH NAWAF AL HAZMI, TAKING REFRESHER TRAINING AT ARIZONA AVIATION.

FBI INVESTIGATORS HAVE SPECULATED THAT AL QAEDA MAY HAVE DIRECTED OTHER EXTREMISTS IN THE PHOENIX AREA TO ENROLL IN AVIATION TRAINING.

BY THE END OF MARCH 2001, HANJOUR HAD COMPLETED HIS TRAINING AND DROVE EAST WITH HAZMI TO AWAIT THE ARRIVAL OF THE "MUSCLE HIJACKERS"––THOSE WHO WOULD STORM THE COCKPITS AND CONTROL THE PASSENGERS.

THE THREE PILOTS IN FLORIDA WERE BY THIS TIME SIMULATING FLIGHTS ON LARGE JETS.

ATTA'S ALLEGED TRIP TO PRAGUE

MUCH HAS BEEN WRITTEN OF ATTA'S ALLEGED TRIP TO PRAGUE AND OF A SUPPOSED MEETING ON APRIL 9, 2001, WITH AN IRAQI INTELLIGENCE OFFICER, AHMAD KHALIL IBRAHIM SAMIR AL ANI. THE COMMISSION BELIEVES IT IS *NOT* SUPPORTED BY AVAILABLE EVIDENCE.
THERE ARE PHOTOS THAT SHOW ATTA IN THE U.S. AT THE TIME, AND HIS CELL PHONE WAS BEING USED. THE ACCUSATION ORIGINATES FROM A SINGLE SOURCE OF THE CZECH INTELLIGENCE SERVICE.

Assembling the Teams

DURING THE SUMMER AND EARLY AUTUMN OF 2000, BIN LADIN AND SENIOR AL QAEDA LEADERS IN AFGHANISTAN STARTED SELECTING THE MUSCLE HIJACKERS.

THESE MEN, DESPITE WHAT THEY WERE CALLED, WERE NOT PHYSICALLY IMPOSING. MOST OF THEM WERE BETWEEN 5' 5" AND 5' 7" IN HEIGHT.

THEY CAME FROM A VARIETY OF EDUCATIONAL AND SOCIETAL BACKGROUNDS.
ALL WERE BETWEEN 20 AND 28, MOST WERE UNEMPLOYED, HAD NO MORE THAN A HIGH SCHOOL EDUCATION, AND WERE UNMARRIED.
TWELVE OF THE THIRTEEN HIJACKERS WERE FROM SAUDI ARABIA.
ONLY FAYEZ BANIHAMMAD CAME FROM THE UAE.

FIVE CAME FROM THE POOR ASIR PROVINCE THAT BORDERS YEMEN.
THIS IS A WEAKLY POLICED AREA SOMETIMES CALLED "THE WILD FRONTIER."

FOUR CAME FROM A CLUSTER OF THREE TOWNS IN THE UNDERDEVELOPED AL-BAHAH REGION AND SHARED A TRIBAL AFFILIATION.

OF THESE FOUR, WALEED AND WAIL AL SHEHRI WERE BROTHERS.
ABDUL AZIZ AL OMARI HAD A UNIVERSITY DEGREE, WAS MARRIED, AND HAD A DAUGHTER.

Map labels: LEBANON, SYRIA, Med. Sea, IRAQ, IRAN, JORDAN, KUWAIT, Tabûk, Dubâ, Halil, Ra's al Khafit, Al Jubayl, Persian, BAHRAIN, Buraydah, Ad Dammâm, Gulf, EGYPT, Medina, Yanbu' al Bahr, Rabigh, RIYADH, Al Hufûf, U.A.E., Jiddah, Mecca, SAUDI ARABIA, Red Sea, Al-Bahah, SUDAN, Asir, "The Wild Frontier", OMAN, Jîzân, Arabian Sea, ERITREA, YEMEN

WALEED AND WAIL AL SHEHRI

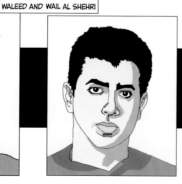

OMARI

ACCORDING TO KSM...

BINALSHIBH, HOWEVER, ARGUED THAT SO MANY WERE SAUDIS BECAUSE AL QAEDA WANTED TO SEND A MESSAGE TO THE GOVERNMENT OF SAUDI ARABIA ABOUT ITS RELATIONSHIP TO THE UNITED STATES.

SO MANY WERE SAUDIS BECAUSE SAUDIS COMPRISED THE LARGEST PORTION OF THE POOL OF RECRUITS.

KSM ESTIMATES THAT IN ANY GIVEN CAMP, 70% OF THE MUJAHIDEEN ARE SAUDIS, 20% ARE YEMENI, AND ONLY 10% COME FROM ELSEWHERE.

MOST SAUDI MUSCLE HIJACKERS DEVELOPED EXTREMIST TIES TWO TO THREE YEARS BEFORE THE ATTACK. THEY WERE TARGETED FOR RECRUITMENT OUTSIDE OF AFGHANISTAN AND PROBABLY IN SAUDI ARABIA ITSELF.

SEVERAL ALSO SPENT TIME IN THE AL QASSIM PROVINCE, THE VERY HEART OF THE STRICT WAHHABI MOVEMENT IN SAUDI ARABIA.

al Qassim Province

Lebanon Syria Iraq
Jordan
Egypt
Iran
Kuwait
Bahrain
Qatar
UAE
Saudi Arabia
Oman
Yemen

RECRUITS CAME THROUGH CONTACTS AT UNIVERSITIES, AT MOSQUES AND, IN A FEW CASES, WITH FAMILY MEMBERS...

...AND A MOSQUE KNOWN BY MODERATE CLERICS AS A "TERRORIST FACTORY."

WHILE TRAINING AT AL QAEDA CAMPS, A DOZEN OF THEM WHO HEARD BIN LADIN'S SPEECHES...

...VOLUNTEERED TO BECOME SUICIDE OPERATIVES AND ENDED UP AS MUSCLE HIJACKERS FOR THE 9/11 OPERATION.

HE IS PERFECT. HE WILL GIVE UP HIS LIFE, HIS RECORD IS CLEAN, AND HE HAS THE PATIENCE OF A DYING MAN.

MOST MUSCLE HIJACKERS UNDERWENT BASIC TRAINING SIMILAR TO THAT OF OTHER RECRUITS.

KSM AND KHALLAD (TAWFIQ BIN ATTASH), BOTH TERRORISTS WHO ARE IN CUSTODY, AGREED ON THE MOST IMPORTANT QUALITIES OF AN AL QAEDA OPERATIVE.

THIS INCLUDED TRAINING IN FIREARMS, HEAVY WEAPONS, EXPLOSIVES, AND TOPOGRAPHY.

THEY ALSO LEARNED DISCIPLINE AND MILITARY LIFE AND WERE SUBJECTED TO ARTIFICIAL STRESSES TO MEASURE THEIR PSYCHOLOGICAL FITNESS AND COMMITMENT TO JIHAD.

THE TRAINEES ALSO BUTCHERED A SHEEP AND A CAMEL TO PREPARE THEM TO USE KNIVES IN THE OPERATION AND...

...WERE TAUGHT TO STORM THE COCKPIT AT THE EARLIEST OPPORTUNITY.

MUSCLE HIJACKERS BEGAN ARRIVING IN THE U.S. IN LATE APRIL 2001.

THEY ENTERED IN FOUR CITIES (MIAMI, ORLANDO, WASHINGTON, DC, AND NEW YORK). BY JULY 4, ALL 19 HIJACKERS WERE IN THE UNITED STATES.

WHILE IN SUDAN, SENIOR MEMBERS OF AL QAEDA MAINTAINED CONTACTS WITH IRAN AND THE IRANIAN-SUPPORTED TERRORIST ORGANIZATION HEZBOLLAH. EVIDENCE WAS FOUND THAT 8 TO 10 SAUDI MUSCLE OPERATIVES TRAVELED IN OR OUT OF IRAN BETWEEN OCTOBER 2000 AND FEBRUARY 2001.

IRAN

HEZBOLLAH

THERE IS STRONG EVIDENCE THAT IRAN FACILITATED THE TRANSIT OF AL QAEDA MEMBERS INTO AND OUT OF AFGHANISTAN BEFORE 9/11.

HOWEVER, NO EVIDENCE WAS FOUND THAT IRAN OR HEZBOLLAH WAS AWARE OF THE PLANNING OF THE 9/11 ATTACK.

Final Strategies and Tactics

DURING THE EARLY SUMMER OF 2001, ATTA, ASSISTED BY SHEHHI, WAS BUSY COORDINATING THE ARRIVAL OF THE MUSCLE HIJACKERS IN SOUTHERN FLORIDA.

THEY PICKED THEM UP AT THE AIRPORTS...

...FOUND THEM PLACES TO STAY AND HELPED THEM TO SETTLE IN THE UNITED STATES.

VACANCY
Florida
MOTEL

THE NEWCOMERS OPENED BANK ACCOUNTS, ACQUIRED MAILBOXES, RENTED CARS.

SOME EVEN JOINED GYMS, PRESUMABLY TO STAY FIT FOR THE OPERATION.

THE THREE HAMBURG PILOTS, ATTA, SHEHHI, AND JARRAH, TOOK THE FIRST OF THEIR CROSS-COUNTRY SURVEILLANCE FLIGHTS EARLY IN THE SUMMER.
EACH TRAVELED FIRST CLASS, ON UNITED AIRLINES, AND ON THE TYPE OF PLANE THEY WOULD EVENTUALLY PILOT.

BOTH JARRAH AND HANJOUR ASKED FLIGHT INSTRUCTORS TO ALLOW THEM TO FLY--AND ONE TIME EACH DID-- THE HUDSON CORRIDOR, A LOW- ALTITUDE "HALLWAY" ALONG THE HUDSON RIVER THAT PASSES NEW YORK LANDMARKS LIKE THE WORLD TRADE CENTER.

N15886

IN LATE MAY 2001, BINALSHIBH MET WITH BIN LADIN AT AN AL QAEDA FACILITY KNOWN AS "COMPOUND SIX" NEAR KANDAHAR. BIN LADIN TOLD HIM TO ADVISE ATTA TO PROCEED AS PLANNED ON THE FOUR DISCUSSED TARGETS...

...THE WORLD TRADE CENTER... THE PENTAGON... THE WHITE HOUSE... AND THE CAPITOL.

ACCORDING TO BINALSHIBH, BIN LADIN SAID HE PREFERRED THE WHITE HOUSE TO THE CAPITOL.

IN JUNE 2001, BINALSHIBH MET KSM IN PAKISTAN, WHERE KSM TOLD HIM TO ASK ATTA TO SELECT A DATE FOR THE ATTACKS.

FINALLY, ON JULY 8, ATTA ARRIVED IN MADRID AND MET BINALSHIBH THE NEXT DAY.

BUSY ORGANIZING THE HIJACKERS, ATTA SAID HE NEEDED FIVE OR SIX WEEKS MORE TO SELECT A DATE FOR THE OPERATION.

ATTA UNDERSTOOD BIN LADIN'S INTEREST IN STRIKING THE WHITE HOUSE, BUT HE BELIEVED THIS TARGET WAS TOO DIFFICULT. HAZMI AND HANJOUR, HOWEVER, WHO HAD FLOWN RECONNAISSANCE FLIGHTS NEAR THE PENTAGON...

...HAD BEEN TASKED TO EVALUATE THE FEASIBILITY.

BOTH ATTA AND SHEHHI WOULD HIT THE TRADE CENTER, HANJOUR THE PENTAGON, AND JARRAH THE CAPITOL.

IF ANY PILOT COULD NOT REACH HIS TARGET, HE WAS TO CRASH HIS PLANE.

ATTA PLANNED TO CRASH HIS ON THE STREETS OF NEW YORK.

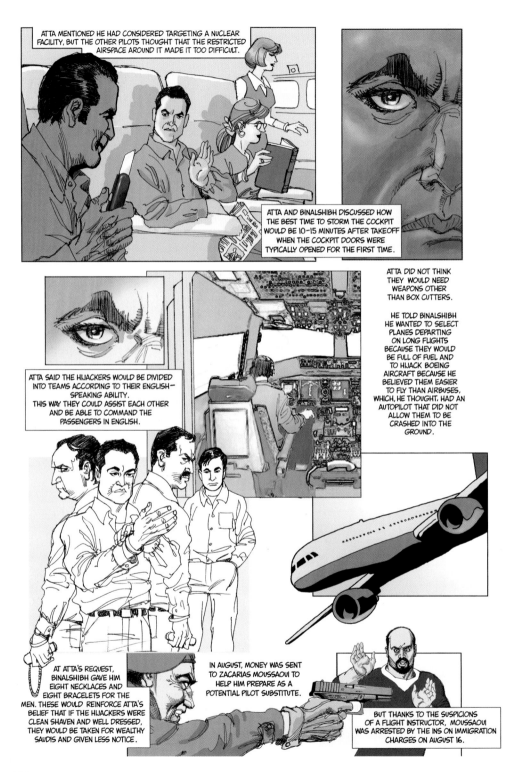

ATTA MENTIONED HE HAD CONSIDERED TARGETING A NUCLEAR FACILITY, BUT THE OTHER PILOTS THOUGHT THAT THE RESTRICTED AIRSPACE AROUND IT MADE IT TOO DIFFICULT.

ATTA AND BINALSHIBH DISCUSSED HOW THE BEST TIME TO STORM THE COCKPIT WOULD BE 10-15 MINUTES AFTER TAKEOFF WHEN THE COCKPIT DOORS WERE TYPICALLY OPENED FOR THE FIRST TIME.

ATTA DID NOT THINK THEY WOULD NEED WEAPONS OTHER THAN BOX CUTTERS.

HE TOLD BINALSHIBH HE WANTED TO SELECT PLANES DEPARTING ON LONG FLIGHTS BECAUSE THEY WOULD BE FULL OF FUEL AND TO HIJACK BOEING AIRCRAFT BECAUSE HE BELIEVED THEM EASIER TO FLY THAN AIRBUSES, WHICH, HE THOUGHT, HAD AN AUTOPILOT THAT DID NOT ALLOW THEM TO BE CRASHED INTO THE GROUND.

ATTA SAID THE HIJACKERS WOULD BE DIVIDED INTO TEAMS ACCORDING TO THEIR ENGLISH-SPEAKING ABILITY.
THIS WAY THEY COULD ASSIST EACH OTHER AND BE ABLE TO COMMAND THE PASSENGERS IN ENGLISH.

AT ATTA'S REQUEST, BINALSHIBH GAVE HIM EIGHT NECKLACES AND EIGHT BRACELETS FOR THE MEN. THESE WOULD REINFORCE ATTA'S BELIEF THAT IF THE HIJACKERS WERE CLEAN SHAVEN AND WELL DRESSED, THEY WOULD BE TAKEN FOR WEALTHY SAUDIS AND GIVEN LESS NOTICE.

IN AUGUST, MONEY WAS SENT TO ZACARIAS MOUSSAOUI TO HELP HIM PREPARE AS A POTENTIAL PILOT SUBSTITUTE.

BUT THANKS TO THE SUSPICIONS OF A FLIGHT INSTRUCTOR, MOUSSAOUI WAS ARRESTED BY THE INS ON IMMIGRATION CHARGES ON AUGUST 16.

ATTA RESPONDED THAT THE WHITE HOUSE WOULD BE STRUCK IF IT PROVED POSSIBLE.

AND THAT THE ATTACKS WOULD NOT HAPPEN TILL CONGRESS RECONVENED IN SEPTEMBER.

IN A SERIES OF COMMUNICATIONS BETWEEN ATTA AND BINALSHIBH IN AUGUST, THE ASSIGNMENTS OF MUSCLE HIJACKERS, THE BEST WAY TO PURCHASE TICKETS, AND THE WHITE HOUSE AS A TARGET WERE ALL DISCUSSED.

BETWEEN AUGUST 25 AND SEPTEMBER 5, ALL 19 TICKETS WERE PURCHASED...

...FOR SEPTEMBER 11!

IT THEREFORE APPEARS THAT THE ATTACK DATE WAS SELECTED BY THE THIRD WEEK OF AUGUST. AND THE MESSAGE, IN CODE, SENT OUT WAS...

...THE 11TH OF SEPTEMBER. (11/9)

AL QAEDA'S LONG-PLANNED ASSASSINATION OF THE NORTHERN ALLIANCE LEADER, AHMED SHAH MASSOUD, TOOK PLACE ON SEPTEMBER 9.

THE TALIBAN OFFENSIVE AGAINST THE NORTHERN ALLIANCE GOT UNDER WAY ON SEPTEMBER 10.

AND ON THE MORNING OF SEPTEMBER 11, 19 HIJACKERS LEFT THEIR HOTEL AND MOTEL ROOMS IN SEVERAL CITIES ON THE NORTHEAST COAST OF THE UNITED STATES.

The
Summer
of Threat

Chapter 8:
"THE SYSTEM WAS BLINKING RED"

AS 2001 BEGAN, COUNTERTERRORISM OFFICIALS WERE RECEIVING FREQUENT BUT FRAGMENTARY REPORTS ABOUT THREATS IN THE U.S. AND TO ITS INTERESTS ABROAD.

INFORMATION WAS GATHERED THROUGH SEVERAL METHODS INCLUDING HUMAN SOURCES.

WE MAY HAVE TROUBLE IN THE DOWNTOWN TUNNEL.

BECAUSE REPORTING IS SO VOLUMINOUS, ONLY A SMALL FRACTION IS CHOSEN FOR BRIEFING THE PRESIDENT AND SENIOR OFFICIALS.

Bin Ladin planning multiple operations

PDB

LESS SENSITIVE REPORTS ARE WIDELY DISSEMINATED TO STATE AND LOCAL ENFORCEMENT AGENCIES.

DURING 2001, CIA DIRECTOR GEORGE TENET MET DAILY WITH PRESIDENT BUSH, WHO WAS BRIEFED BY THE CIA ON WHAT IS KNOWN AS THE PRESIDENT'S DAILY BRIEF (PDB).

EACH PDB CONSISTS OF A SERIES OF 6-8 BRIEFS ON A BROAD ARRAY OF TOPICS.

THERE WERE MORE THAN 40 INTELLIGENCE ARTICLES IN THE PDBS RELATING TO BIN LADIN FROM JANUARY 20 TO SEPTEMBER 10, 2001.

IN THE SPRING OF 2001, THE LEVEL OF REPORTING ON TERRORIST THREATS AND PLANNED ATTACKS REACHED THE HIGHEST LEVEL SINCE THE MILLENNIUM ALERT.

HE ALSO WARNED OF TERRORIST CELLS IN THE U.S., INCLUDING AL QAEDA.

CLARKE WARNED NSA ADVISER RICE OF A POSSIBLE TRUCK BOMB ASSAULT ON THE WHITE HOUSE.

THERE WAS ALSO A THREAT OF AN ATTACK IN ISRAEL, SAUDI ARABIA, OR INDIA.

ON APRIL 13, IN RESPONSE TO THESE THREATS, THE FBI SENT A MESSAGE TO ALL ITS FIELD OFFICES...

WE'RE TO TASK ALL RESOURCES TO GET INFORMATION ON CURRENT OPERATIONAL ACTIVITIES RELATING TO SUNNI EXTREMISM.

ON APRIL 20, TOP OFFICIALS WERE BRIEFED ON THE POSSIBLE DOINGS OF ABU ZUBAYDAH, A MAJOR AL QAEDA FIGURE.

BIN LADIN IS PLANNING MULTIPLE OPERATIONS.

AND ON APRIL 30, A MEETING OF DEPUTIES BEGAN WITH THIS BRIEFING.

IN MAY, THE DRUMBEAT GREW LOUDER.

AT THAT TIME, RICHARD CLARKE WROTE TO RICE AND HER DEPUTY, STEPHEN HADLEY.

memo:
When these attacks occur, as they likely will, we will wonder what more we could have done to stop them.

BIN LADIN PUBLIC PROFILE MAY PRESAGE ATTACKS

PLAN TO LAUNCH ATTACKS ON LONDON, BOSTON, NEW YORK

POSSIBLE HOSTAGE ATTACK ON AMERICANS ABROAD

CELL IN CANADA PLANNING U.S. ATTACK

MANY OF THESE REPORTS WERE MADE AVAILABLE TO THE PRESIDENT, THE VICE PRESIDENT, AND NSA ADVISER RICE.

REPORTS OF THREATS SURGED IN JUNE AND JULY.

KSM IS REPORTED TO BE RECRUITING PEOPLE TO GO TO THE U.S. AND JOIN COLLEAGUES ALREADY THERE...

...SO THEY MIGHT CONDUCT TERRORIST ATTACKS ON BIN LADIN'S BEHALF.

AN ARTICLE IN THE AUGUST 6 PDB TITLED "BIN LADIN DETERMINED TO STRIKE IN THE U.S." WAS THE 36TH ITEM BRIEFED THAT YEAR RELATED TO BIN LADIN OR AL QAEDA, AND THE FIRST DEVOTED TO THE POSSIBILITIES OF AN ATTACK IN THE U.S.

PDB

Bin Ladin determined to strike in the U.S.

THE FOLLOWING DAY'S SENIOR EXECUTIVE INTELLIGENCE BRIEF (SEIB) REPEATED THE TITLE BUT DID NOT CONTAIN MANY MAJOR POINTS, INCLUDING THE ALLEGED CASING OF N.Y. BUILDINGS AND THAT THE FBI HAD APPROXIMATELY 70 ONGOING BIN LADIN-RELATED INVESTIGATIONS.

PRESIDENT BUSH TOLD THE COMMISSION THAT THE AUGUST 6 REPORT WAS HISTORICAL IN NATURE. IT INFORMED HIM THAT AL QAEDA WAS DANGEROUS, WHICH HE ALREADY KNEW. HE DID NOT RECALL DISCUSSING THE REPORT WITH THE ATTORNEY GENERAL OR WHETHER RICE HAD DONE SO.
HE SAID IF HE HAD BEEN ADVISED THAT THERE WAS A CELL IN THE U.S., HE WOULD HAVE MOVED TO TAKE CARE OF IT.

OVERSEAS, NUMEROUS ACTIONS WERE TAKEN TO COUNTER THREATS.

PLEASE MOVE ON. WE'RE CLOSING THE EMBASSY.

FAR LESS WAS DONE DOMESTICALLY, PERHAPS BECAUSE THE THREATS WERE VAGUE.

ALTHOUGH THE FAA HAD AUTHORITY TO ISSUE SECURITY DIRECTIVES, NONE RELEASED THAT SUMMER INCREASED SECURITY AT CHECKPOINTS OR ON BOARD AIRCRAFT.

MOST CIRCULARS URGED CARRIERS TO "EXERCISE PRUDENCE."

WHATEVER THAT MEANS.

IN SUM, THE DOMESTIC AGENCIES NEVER MOBILIZED IN RESPONSE TO THE THREAT. THEY DID NOT HAVE DIRECTION OR A PLAN TO INSTITUTE. THE PUBLIC WAS NOT WARNED.

Late Leads: Mihdhar, Moussaoui, and KSM

ON 4 OCCASIONS IN 2001, THE CIA, THE FBI, OR BOTH HAD APPARENT OPPORTUNITIES TO REFOCUS ON THE SIGNIFICANCE OF HAZMI AND MIHDHAR AND REINVIGORATE THE SEARCH FOR THEM.

THE CIA BELIEVED THAT KHALLAD (TAWFIQ BIN ATTASH), WHO DIRECTED THE COLE BOMBING, AND KHALID AL MIHDHAR, WERE THE SAME MAN.

WHEN MIHDHAR'S PHOTO, TAKEN AT A MEETING IN KUALA LUMPUR, WAS SHOWN TO A CIA SOURCE IN JANUARY 2001...

THIS IS NOT KHALLAD!

YET THE COMMISSION FOUND NO CIA EFFORT TO RENEW THE SEARCH FOR MIHDHAR AND HIS COMPANION OR TO TELL THE FBI OF ITS FINDINGS. IF IT HAD, MIHDHAR MIGHT HAVE BEEN FOUND.

THEY'RE TWO DIFFERENT PEOPLE! BUT THERE'S A LINK BETWEEN THE TWO.

SOMETHING BAD IS DEFINITELY UP, DAVE.

BUT OUR CONCERN IS SOUTHEAST ASIA, NOT THE U.S.

"JOHN," A CIA OFFICIAL, BEGAN A LENGTHY EXCHANGE WITH "DAVE," A CIA ANALYST, ON MAY 15, 2001, ABOUT THE KUALA LUMPUR TRAVELS OF MIHDHAR AND HIS ASSOCIATES AND SOME CABLES FROM 2000.

THE CIA IS AN AGENCY THAT PLAYS ZONE DEFENSE.

THE GUYS AT FBI TEND TO PLAY MAN—TO—MAN AND FOLLOW A CASE TO ITS ENDING.

"JANE," AN FBI ANALYST, WENT TO NEW YORK ON JUNE 11 WITH "DAVE" TO MEET OTHER AGENTS ABOUT THE COLE CASE. AT ONE POINT, SHE SHOWED THEM PHOTOS THAT "JOHN" HAD GIVEN HER.

THESE WERE TAKEN IN MALAYSIA. DO YOU RECOGNIZE FAHD AL QUSO, THE GUY YOU'RE TRACKING, IN ANY OF THEM?

TO HELL WITH THAT. WHO ARE THESE GUYS? WHY WERE THEY BEING FOLLOWED?

HAD THE INFORMATION BEEN SHARED WITH THE FBI, A COMBINATION OF THE TWO DEFENSES MIGHT HAVE BEEN PRODUCTIVE.

I'M NOT AUTHORIZED TO TELL YOU.

DAVE REMAINED QUIET.

HE SAID HE WAS NOT AUTHORIZED TO ANSWER FBI QUESTIONS REGARDING CIA INFORMATION.

"JANE" TOLD THE COMMISSION...

I ASSUMED THAT IF DAVE KNEW THE ANSWERS, HE WOULD HAVE VOLUNTEERED THEM.

THUS THE NEW YORK AGENTS LEFT THE MEETING WITHOUT ANY INFORMATION THAT MIGHT HAVE STARTED THEM LOOKING FOR MIHDHAR.

ON AUGUST 22, "MARY" AND "JANE," BOTH FBI ANALYSTS, REQUESTED THAT MIHDHAR AND HAZMI BE PUT ON THE *TIPOFF* WATCH LIST.

SHOULD THIS BE CLASSIFIED AS AN INTELLIGENCE OPERATION OR A CRIMINAL ONE?

EACH HAS ITS OWN SET OF RULES.

THERE WAS A TOTAL MISUNDERSTANDING OF THE COMPLEX RULES THAT COULD APPLY TO THIS SITUATION.

SOMEDAY SOMEONE WILL DIE-- AND WALL OR NOT-- THE PUBLIC WILL NOT UNDERSTAND WHY WE WERE NOT MORE EFFECTIVE IN THROWING EVERY RESOURCE WE HAD AT CERTAIN PROBLEMS.

AS A RESULT OF THIS CONFUSION, CRIMINAL AGENTS MORE KNOWLEDGEABLE ABOUT AL QAEDA AND CRIMINAL INVESTIGATIVE TECHNIQUES WERE EXCLUDED FROM THE SEARCH.

TAXI STAND

TWO DAYS AFTER THE CIA-FBI MEETING IN NEW YORK, MIHDHAR GOT A NEW U.S. VISA. HE ARRIVED IN NEW YORK CITY ON JULY 4.

NO ONE WAS LOOKING FOR HIM.

COMMISSION MEMBERS FOUND...

"WE BELIEVE THAT IF MORE RESOURCES HAD BEEN APPLIED AND A SIGNIFICANTLY DIFFERENT APPROACH TAKEN, MIHDHAR AND HAZMI MIGHT HAVE BEEN FOUND."

"BOTH COULD HAVE BEEN HELD FOR IMMIGRATION VIOLATIONS OR AS MATERIAL WITNESSES IN THE COLE BOMBING CASE."

"THE SIMPLE FACT OF THEIR DETENTION COULD HAVE DERAILED THE PLAN."

AFTER THE 9/11 ATTACK, THE BRITISH DID FIND...

MOUSSAOUI DID ATTEND AN AL QAEDA TRAINING CAMP IN AFGHANISTAN. IT'S BEEN SUBSTANTIATED. HAD THIS BEEN KNOWN BEFORE, PUBLICITY ABOUT THE CASE MIGHT HAVE DERAILED THE PLOT.

WITH TIME, THE SEARCH FOR MIHDHAR AND HAZMI MIGHT HAVE LED TO A BREAKTHROUGH.

KHALID SHEIKH MOHAMMED, WHO HAD BEEN INDICTED IN JANUARY 1996 FOR HIS ROLE IN THE MANILA AIR PLOT, WAS NOT CONSIDERED A PART OF AL QAEDA BEFORE 9/11. RESPONSIBILITY FOR HIM WAS NOT WITH THE BIN LADIN UNIT BUT THE EXTREMIST BRANCH OF THE COUNTER-TERRORIST CENTER.

BECAUSE HE HAD ALREADY BEEN INDICTED, HE BECAME TARGETED FOR ARREST.

HE'S GONE!

ANOTHER TIP BLOWN.

RESPONSIBILITY FOR KSM WAS TRANSFERRED TO THE RENDITIONS BRANCH OF THE COUNTERTERRORIST CENTER.

IN SEPTEMBER 2000, A SOURCE REPORTED...

I CAN TELL YOU THAT A MAN NAMED KHALID AL-SHAYKH AL-BALLUSHI IS A KEY LIEUTENANT IN AL QAEDA.

"AL-BALLUSHI" MEANS "FROM BALUCHISTAN"... AND KSM IS FROM BALUCHISTAN.

IN APRIL 2001, THE CIA FOUND...

SOMEONE NAMED MUKHTAR IS ASSOCIATED WITH AL QAEDA LIEUTENANT ABU ZUBAYDAH AND IS INVOLVED IN THE PLANNING OF TERRORIST ACTIVITIES.

ON JUNE 12, 2001, A CIA REPORT SAID...

THIS "KHALED" IS ACTIVELY RECRUITING PEOPLE TO TRAVEL OUTSIDE AFGHANISTAN, INCLUDING THE U.S., WHERE COLLEAGUES ARE ALREADY THERE TO CARRY OUT TERRORIST ACTIVITY.

COULD KHALED BE KHALID SHEIKH MOHAMMED?

ON AUGUST 28, 2001, THE BIN LADIN UNIT LEARNED THAT KSM'S NICKNAME WAS MUKHTAR, BUT THE U.S. GOVERNMENT WAS ONCE AGAIN UNABLE TO CONNECT THE DOTS.

TWO WEEKS BEFORE 9/11, THE BIN LADIN UNIT LEARNED THIS WAS TRUE. BUT THE U.S. GOVERNMENT COULD NOT FIT THE PIECES OF THE PUZZLE TOGETHER. THEN TIME RAN OUT.

Chapter 9: HEROISM AND HORROR

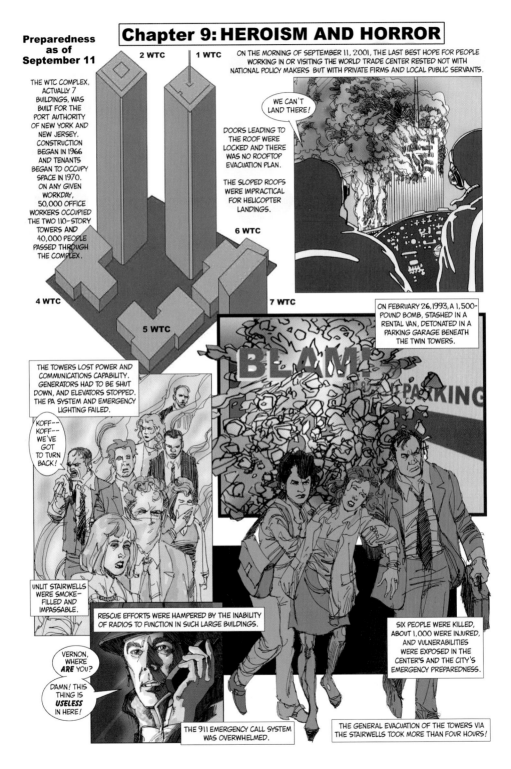

2 WTC **1 WTC**

ON THE MORNING OF SEPTEMBER 11, 2001, THE LAST BEST HOPE FOR PEOPLE WORKING IN OR VISITING THE WORLD TRADE CENTER RESTED NOT WITH NATIONAL POLICY MAKERS BUT WITH PRIVATE FIRMS AND LOCAL PUBLIC SERVANTS.

THE WTC COMPLEX, ACTUALLY 7 BUILDINGS, WAS BUILT FOR THE PORT AUTHORITY OF NEW YORK AND NEW JERSEY. CONSTRUCTION BEGAN IN 1966 AND TENANTS BEGAN TO OCCUPY SPACE IN 1970. ON ANY GIVEN WORKDAY, 50,000 OFFICE WORKERS OCCUPIED THE TWO 110-STORY TOWERS AND 40,000 PEOPLE PASSED THROUGH THE COMPLEX.

WE CAN'T LAND THERE!

DOORS LEADING TO THE ROOF WERE LOCKED AND THERE WAS NO ROOFTOP EVACUATION PLAN.

THE SLOPED ROOFS WERE IMPRACTICAL FOR HELICOPTER LANDINGS.

6 WTC

4 WTC

5 WTC

7 WTC

ON FEBRUARY 26, 1993, A 1,500-POUND BOMB, STASHED IN A RENTAL VAN, DETONATED IN A PARKING GARAGE BENEATH THE TWIN TOWERS.

THE TOWERS LOST POWER AND COMMUNICATIONS CAPABILITY. GENERATORS HAD TO BE SHUT DOWN, AND ELEVATORS STOPPED. THE PA SYSTEM AND EMERGENCY LIGHTING FAILED.

KOFF-- KOFF-- WE'VE GOT TO TURN BACK!

BEAM PARKING

UNLIT STAIRWELLS WERE SMOKE-FILLED AND IMPASSABLE.

RESCUE EFFORTS WERE HAMPERED BY THE INABILITY OF RADIOS TO FUNCTION IN SUCH LARGE BUILDINGS.

SIX PEOPLE WERE KILLED, ABOUT 1,000 WERE INJURED, AND VULNERABILITIES WERE EXPOSED IN THE CENTER'S AND THE CITY'S EMERGENCY PREPAREDNESS.

VERNON, WHERE *ARE* YOU?

DAMN! THIS THING IS *USELESS* IN HERE!

THE 911 EMERGENCY CALL SYSTEM WAS OVERWHELMED.

THE GENERAL EVACUATION OF THE TOWERS VIA THE STAIRWELLS TOOK MORE THAN FOUR HOURS!

TO ADDRESS THE PROBLEMS ENCOUNTERED BY THE 1993 BOMBING, THE PORT AUTHORITY SPENT $100 MILLION TO MAKE PHYSICAL, STRUCTURAL, AND TECHNOLOGICAL IMPROVEMENTS TO THE WTC AND TO ENHANCE FIRE SAFETY. BUT...

WHY THE HECK DIDN'T THEY TELL US?

DOOR TO ROOF

THIS IS A LOCKED DOOR

FULL OR PARTIAL EVACUATIONS WERE **NOT** HELD.

THEY WERE NEVER TOLD NOT TO EVACUATE UP.

OR THAT ROOF DOORS WERE KEPT LOCKED AND ROOFTOP EVACUATIONS WERE **NOT** PART OF THE PLAN.

DAMN! THERE'S SOMETHING GOING ON AT THE TWIN TOWERS!

WE'RE IN BROOKLYN HEIGHTS, BUT WE'LL GET TO LOWER MANHATTAN IN 15 MINUTES.

ON 9/11, THE PORT AUTHORITY POLICE DEPARTMENT OF 1,331 OFFICERS COVERED 9 FACILITIES AND LACKED ANY PROCEDURE OR REAL ABILITY FOR ONE FACILITY TO CONTACT ANOTHER.

BUT THIS RADIO CAN'T REACH THEM!

THE 40-THOUSAND-OFFICER NYPD WAS DIVIDED INTO 35 DIFFERENT RADIO ZONES. OFFICERS HAD PORTABLE RADIOS WITH 20 OR MORE CHANNELS SO THEY COULD ANSWER CALLS OUT OF THEIR PRECINCT.

THE 11,000-MEMBER FIRE DEPARTMENT OF NEW YORK WAS ORGANIZED INTO 9 SEPARATE GEOGRAPHIC DIVISIONS.

HELLO? HELLO! NOW I CAN'T REACH HIM INSIDE THAT BLASTED PLACE!

THEIR RADIOS PERFORMED POORLY IN 1993, AS SIGNALS DID NOT OFTEN PENETRATE STEEL AND CONCRETE FLOORS AND TOO MANY USED THEME COMMUNICATIONS CHANNELS.

THE PORT AUTHORITY, AT ITS OWN EXPENSE, INSTALLED A REPEATER SYSTEM IN 1994 TO ENHANCE THE FDNY'S RADIO COMMUNICATIONS IN THE TOWER.

IN 1996, MAYOR GIULIANI CREATED THE OFFICE OF EMERGENCY MANAGEMENT (OEM) TO MONITOR THE CITY'S KEY COMMUNICATIONS CHANNELS, TO IMPROVE THE CITY'S RESPONSE TO MAJOR INCIDENTS, AND TO PLAY A CRUCIAL ROLE IN MANAGING THE CITY'S OVERALL RESPONSE TO AN INCIDENT.

HOWEVER, AS OF 9/11, THE CITY WAS NOT PREPARED TO COMPREHENSIVELY COORDINATE EFFORTS IN RESPONDING TO A MAJOR INCIDENT. THE OEM HAD NOT OVERCOME THIS PROBLEM.

AT 8:46:40, HIJACKED AMERICAN AIRLINES FLIGHT 11 FLEW INTO THE UPPER PORTION OF THE NORTH TOWER, CUTTING THROUGH FLOORS 93 TO 99.

A JET FUEL FIREBALL ERUPTED UPON IMPACT AND SHOT DOWN AT LEAST ONE BANK OF ELEVATORS.

THE FIREBALL EXPLODED ONTO NUMEROUS FLOORS, INCLUDING THE 77TH, THE 22ND, THE LOBBY LEVEL, AND FOUR STORIES BELOW.

SHOOM!

EVIDENCE SUGGESTS THAT ALL THREE OF THE BUILDING'S STAIRWELLS BECAME IMPASSABLE FROM THE 92ND FLOOR UP.

HUNDREDS WERE KILLED INSTANTLY BY THE IMPACT.

HUNDREDS MORE REMAINED ALIVE BUT TRAPPED.

THE BURNING JET FUEL IMMEDIATELY CREATED THICK BLACK SMOKE THAT ENVELOPED THE UPPER FLOORS OF THE NORTH TOWER. THE ROOF OF THE SOUTH TOWER WAS ALSO ENGULFED IN SMOKE BECAUSE OF THE PREVAILING WINDS.

HUNDREDS OF CIVILIANS TRAPPED ON OR ABOVE THE 92ND FLOOR GATHERED IN LARGE AND SMALL GROUPS BETWEEN THE 103RD AND 106TH FLOORS.

CIVILIANS WERE TRAPPED IN ELEVATORS, WHILE OTHERS BELOW THE IMPACT ZONE WERE TRAPPED OR WAITING FOR ASSISTANCE.

EVACUATE IMMEDIATELY!

IT IS UNCLEAR WHEN THE FIRST FULL BUILDING EVACUATION ORDER WAS ATTEMPTED OVER THE PUBLIC-ADDRESS SYSTEM.

HOW?

BUT BECAUSE OF DAMAGE TO BUILDING SYSTEMS FROM THE PLANE'S IMPACT, WHEN THE ORDER WAS GIVEN IT WAS NOT HEARD IN MANY LOCATIONS.

RINNG! RIIINGG! RIIINNG!

THE 911 PHONE SYSTEM IS SWAMPED!

HOLD ON, PLEASE!

THE 911 SYSTEM WAS NOT EQUIPPED TO HANDLE THE ENORMOUS VOLUME OF CALLS THAT CAME IN BECAUSE OF THE PLANE CRASH.

OPERATORS COULD ALSO NOT KNOWLEDGEABLY ADVISE CALLERS IN THE BUILDING. TOO MANY WERE TOLD TO SIT TIGHT AND WAIT FOR HELP.

WE'VE GOT TO GET EVERYONE OUT OF THERE THAT WE CAN!

AND FROM THE OTHER TOWER, TOO.

BY 8:57, THEY HAD INSTRUCTED THE PORT AUTHORITY POLICE AND BUILDING PERSONNEL TO EVACUATE THE SOUTH TOWER AS WELL.

LET'S MOVE, FOLKS. QUICKLY BUT ORDERLY.

IN THE SOUTH TOWER, THE 20 FLOORS OF MORGAN STANLEY WERE EVACUATED BY DECISION OF COMPANY SECURITY OFFICIALS.

FDNY CHIEFS IN THE NORTH TOWER LOBBY DETERMINED AT ONCE THAT ALL BUILDING OCCUPANTS SHOULD ATTEMPT TO EVACUATE IMMEDIATELY.

RECEIVING CONFLICTING SUGGESTIONS, MOST SOUTH TOWER TENANTS STAYED WHERE THEY WERE. CLEARLY, THE PROSPECT OF ANOTHER PLANE HITTING THE SECOND BUILDING WAS BEYOND CONTEMPLATION.

THE FDNY RESPONSE BEGAN WITHIN FIVE SECONDS OF THE CRASH. AS OF 9:00, 235 FIREFIGHTERS, 21 ENGINE COMPANIES, 9 LADDER COMPANIES...

...4 ELITE RESCUE TEAMS, 1 HAZMAT TEAM, AND SUPPORT HAD BEEN DISPATCHED.

WHEE-OOO!

AND 9 BROOKLYN UNITS WERE STAGED ON THE BROOKLYN SIDE OF THE BROOKLYN-BATTERY TUNNEL AWAITING ORDERS.

AT 8:52, FIREFIGHTERS ENCOUNTERED BADLY BURNED CIVILIANS, BLOWN-OUT WINDOWS, AND OTHER DAMAGE, AND QUICKLY LEARNED THAT ALL ELEVATORS WERE INOPERABLE.

THEY KNEW AT ONCE THIS WOULD BE A RESCUE OPERATION, NOT A FIREFIGHTING ONE.

AT 8:57, ONE ENGINE AND ONE LADDER COMPANY BEGAN CLIMBING STAIRWELL C AS THE CHIEFS BEGAN TO FORMULATE A PLAN.

THEY ASKED POLICE AND WTC PERSONNEL TO EVACUATE THE SOUTH TOWER, BELIEVING THE CRASH MADE THE ENTIRE COMPLEX UNSAFE.

NYPD POLICE

AT 8:58, THE NYPD CHIEF OF DEPARTMENT RAISED THE MOBILIZATION LEVEL TO 4, SENDING APPROXIMATELY 22 LIEUTENANTS, 100 SERGEANTS, AND 800 POLICE OFFICERS FROM ALL OVER TO THE SCENE.

THEY IMMEDIATELY BEGAN RESCUE WORK AND CLEARING MAJOR THOROUGHFARES. TRANSIT POLICE SHUT DOWN SUBWAY STATIONS IN THE AREA. THIS WAS THE LARGEST RESCUE OPERATION IN THE CITY'S HISTORY. OVER 1,000 FIRST RESPONDERS HAD BEEN DEPLOYED AND EVACUATION HAD BEGUN.

THEN THE SECOND PLANE HIT.

AT 9:03:11, THE HIJACKED UNITED FLIGHT 175 HIT THE SOUTH TOWER FROM THE SOUTH, CRASHING THROUGH THE 77TH TO 85TH FLOORS. AND THE MOST COMPLICATED RESCUE OPERATION IN HISTORY INSTANTLY DOUBLED IN MAGNITUDE.

THE PLANE BANKED AS IT HIT THE BUILDING, LEAVING PORTIONS OF THE STRUCTURE UNDAMAGED ON IMPACT FLOORS.

AS A CONSEQUENCE, ONE OF THE STAIRWELLS INITIALLY REMAINED PASSABLE FROM THE 91ST FLOOR DOWN.

AT THE LOWER END OF THE IMPACT, THE 78TH FLOOR, HUNDREDS HAD BEEN WAITING TO EVACUATE WHEN THE PLANE HIT.

MANY WERE KILLED OR SEVERELY INJURED; OTHERS WERE RELATIVELY UNHARMED.

MANY IN AND ABOVE THE IMPACT ZONE ASCENDED THE STAIRS. SOME FOUND FLOORS IN FLAMES WHILE OTHERS WERE STYMIED BY LOCKED OR JAMMED DOORS.

BUT BY THE LOWER 70'S, STAIRWELLS A AND B WERE WELL LIT AND CONDITIONS GENERALLY NORMAL.

BY 9:35, THE WEST STREET LOBBY OF THE SOUTH TOWER WAS BECOMING OVERWHELMED BY INJURED PEOPLE WHO HAD DESCENDED TO THE LOBBY.

MEANWHILE, IN THE NORTH TOWER, TRAPPED CIVILIANS WERE RECEIVING CONFLICTING ADVICE ABOUT WHETHER TO STAY PUT OR DESCEND.

AMBULANCE

MOST WHO DESCENDED LATE DIED WHEN THE TOWER COLLAPSED.

BY 9:15, THE NUMBER OF FDNY PERSONNEL EN ROUTE TO OR PRESENT AT THE SCENE WAS FAR GREATER THAN THE CHIEFS HAD REQUESTED.

FIRE COMPANIES HAD DISPATCHED MORE MEN THAN HAD BEEN REQUESTED AND SEVERAL UNITS HAD SELF-DISPATCHED.

FIRE COMPANIES BEGAN TO ASCEND STAIRWELL B IN THE NORTH TOWER AT ABOUT 9:07, LADEN WITH ABOUT 100 POUNDS OF PROTECTIVE CLOTHING, BREATHING APPARATUS, AND EQUIPMENT.

LET'S SEE IF ANYONE IS STILL HERE.

EVERYONE HERE? TRY NOT TO GET SEPARATED.

F·6 FDNY

IN THEIR ASCENT, THEY PASSED A STEADY AND HEAVY STREAM OF DESCENDING CIVILIANS AND WERE IMPRESSED BY THEIR LACK OF PANIC.

JUST PRIOR TO 10:00, ONE ENGINE COMPANY HAD REACHED THE 54TH FLOOR, AT LEAST TWO OTHERS HAD REACHED THE 44TH, AND NUMEROUS OTHERS WERE BETWEEN THE 5TH AND 37TH.

BY 9:30, CHIEFS IN CHARGE OF THE SOUTH TOWER WERE STILL IN NEED OF ADDITIONAL COMPANIES. IMPORTANT FACTORS FOR THIS WERE CONFUSION AS TO WHICH TOWER WAS WHICH AND HOW TO REACH IT.

A SECOND ALARM WAS REQUESTED AT 9:37. BY 9:58, FIREFIGHTERS HAD REACHED THE 78TH FLOOR, FINDING GREAT DESTRUCTION AND NUMEROUS FATALITIES.

TO THE KNOWLEDGE OF THE COMMISSION, NONE OF THE CHIEFS PRESENT BELIEVED THAT A TOTAL COLLAPSE OF EITHER TOWER WAS POSSIBLE.

BUT AT ABOUT 9:57, AN ENGINEER REMARKED THAT THE TWIN TOWERS WERE IN IMMINENT DANGER OF TOTAL COLLAPSE.

IMMEDIATELY AFTER THE SECOND PLANE HIT, THE NYPD ORDERED A SECOND LEVEL-4 MOBILIZATION, BRINGING THE TOTAL NUMBER OF OFFICERS RESPONDING TO CLOSE TO 2,000.

THE FIRST NYPD EMERGENCY SERVICE TEAM ENTERED THE NORTH TOWER AT ABOUT 9:15. SEVERAL MORE TEAMS SOON ENTERED AND ASCENDED THE TOWER TO SUPPORT FDNY PERSONNEL.

BY 9:50, THE LEAD TEAM HAD REACHED THE 31ST FLOOR. THERE APPEARED TO BE NO MORE CIVILIANS DESCENDING, BUT THEY DID TREAT EXHAUSTED FIREFIGHTERS.

AT 9:59, THE SOUTH TOWER COLLAPSED IN TEN SECONDS, KILLING ALL CIVILIANS AND EMERGENCY PERSONNEL INSIDE...

AS WELL AS A NUMBER OF INDIVIDUALS-- BOTH RESPONDERS AND CIVILIANS-- IN THE CONCOURSE, IN THE MARRIOTT, AND ON NEIGHBORING STREETS.

WE CAN'T GET THROUGH ANY LONGER!

THE FDNY OVERALL COMMAND POST, AND POSTS IN THE NORTH TOWER LOBBY, THE MARRIOTT LOBBY, AND THE STAGING AREA ON WEST STREET, ALL CEASED TO OPERATE BECAUSE OF THEIR PROXIMITY TO THE BUILDING.

I HEAR SOMETHING.

YOU'RE ALWAYS HEARING SOMETHING.

THOSE WHO HAD BEEN IN THE NORTH LOBBY HAD NO WAY OF KNOWING THAT THE SOUTH TOWER HAD COLLAPSED.

NEITHER DID THOSE WHO WERE NOT NEAR OPEN WINDOWS ON THE UPPER FLOORS.

DESPITE HIS LACK OF KNOWLEDGE OF THE COLLAPSE, A CHIEF IN THE PROCESS OF EVACUATING THE NORTH TOWER ORDERED:

WE'VE GOT TO LEAVE! THIS TOWER COULD FALL!

SIMILAR ORDERS WERE GIVEN ON OTHER FLOORS.

THE MARRIOTT HOTEL SUFFERED SIGNIFICANT DAMAGE IN THE COLLAPSE OF THE SOUTH TOWER. THOSE IN THE LOBBY WERE KNOCKED DOWN AND ENVELOPED IN THE DARKNESS OF A DEBRIS CLOUD.

UP ABOVE,
FOUR COMPANIES WERE DESCENDING THE STAIRS SINGLE FILE IN A LINE OF APPROXIMATELY 20 MEN.
FOUR SURVIVED.

THAT BUILDING SHOULD BE A GONER.

AT 10:04, NYPD AVIATION REPORTED THAT THE TOP FIFTEEN STORIES OF THE NORTH TOWER WERE "GLOWING RED" AND THAT THEY MIGHT COLLAPSE.

THIS DID NOT STOP POLICE AND FIREFIGHTERS FROM SEARCHING FOR SURVIVORS AND AIDING CIVILIANS TO SAFETY.
AS TIME GREW SHORT AND DESPERATE, CIVILIANS LEAPED FROM NORTH TOWER UPPER FLOORS.

THE NORTH TOWER COLLAPSED AT 10:28:25, KILLING ALL CIVILIANS STILL ALIVE ON UPPER FLOORS, AN UNDETERMINED NUMBER BELOW, AND SCORES OF FIRST RESPONDERS.

Emergency Response at the Pentagon

IF IT HAD HAPPENED ON ANY OTHER DAY, THE DISASTER AT THE PENTAGON WOULD BE REMEMBERED AS A SINGULAR CHALLENGE AND AN EXTRAORDINARY NATIONAL STORY.
BUT THE CALAMITY AT THE WORLD TRADE CENTER THAT SAME MORNING, WHICH INSTANTLY IMPERILED TENS OF THOUSANDS, MADE THE TWO EXPERIENCES NOT COMPARABLE.
NEVERTHELESS, THERE ARE LESSONS IN THE RESPONSE AT THE PENTAGON.

METRO ENTRANCE

AT 9:37, THE WEST WALL OF THE PENTAGON WAS HIT BY HIJACKED AMERICAN FLIGHT 77...

RIVER ENTRANCE

...KILLING ALL 64 PEOPLE ABOARD AS WELL AS 125 PEOPLE INSIDE THE PENTAGON.

MALL ENTRANCE

LOCAL, STATE, AND FEDERAL AGENCIES IMMEDIATELY RESPONDED AND WERE EFFECTIVE.

THE INHERENT COMPLICATIONS OF RESPONSE ACROSS JURISDICTIONS WERE OVERCOME BECAUSE OF THE INCIDENT COMMAND SYSTEM, A MANAGEMENT STRUCTURE FOR EMERGENCY RESPONSE THAT WAS IN PLACE IN THE NATIONAL CAPITAL REGION.

SEVERAL FACTORS DISTINGUISH THIS RESPONSE FROM THAT IN NEW YORK. THIS WAS A SINGLE INCIDENT AND IT WAS NOT 1,000 FEET ABOVE THE GROUND.
THE INCIDENT SITE WAS RELATIVELY EASY TO SECURE, AND THERE WERE NO OTHER BUILDINGS IN THE AREA.

YET THERE WERE SIGNIFICANT PROBLEMS WITH SELF-DISPATCHING AND COMMUNICATIONS, ECHOING THOSE EXPERIENCES IN NEW YORK.

Analysis

IN NEW YORK, THE FDNY, NYPD, THE PORT AUTHORITY, WTC EMPLOYEES, AND THE WTC OCCUPANTS THEMSELVES DID THEIR BEST TO COPE WITH AN UNIMAGINABLE CATASTROPHE FOR WHICH THEY WERE UNPREPARED IN TERMS OF TRAINING AND MIND-SET.

IT HAS BEEN ESTIMATED THAT BETWEEN 16,400 AND 18,800 CIVILIANS WERE IN THE WTC AS OF 8:46 ON SEPTEMBER 11. AT MOST, 2,152 INDIVIDUALS DIED AT THE WTC COMPLEX WHO WERE NOT RESCUE WORKERS OR ON THE TWO PLANES.

OUT OF THIS NUMBER, 1,942 WERE AT OR ABOVE THE IMPACT ZONES. THIS DATA STRONGLY SUPPORTS THAT THE EVACUATION WAS A SUCCESS FOR CIVILIANS BELOW THE IMPACT.

THE EVACUATION WAS AIDED BY CHANGES MADE BY THE PORT AUTHORITY IN RESPONSE TO THE 1993 BOMBING, REDUCING EVACUATION TIME FROM MORE THAN FOUR HOURS TO UNDER AN HOUR ON SEPTEMBER 11.

WE'VE GOT TO GET OUT OF HERE!

THE "FIRST" RESPONDERS ON 9/11 WERE PRIVATE-SECTOR CIVILIANS. BECAUSE 85% OF OUR NATION'S INFRASTRUCTURE IS CONTROLLED BY THE PRIVATE SECTOR, CIVILIANS ARE LIKELY TO BE THE FIRST RESPONDERS IN ANY FUTURE CATASTROPHE. THEREFORE, THE COMMISSION MAKES THE FOLLOWING CONCLUSIONS.

THE CIVILIANS AT OR ABOVE THE IMPACT ZONE HAD THE SMALLEST HOPE OF SURVIVAL. THEIR ONLY HOPE WAS A SWIFT AIR RESCUE, BUT THIS WAS IMPOSSIBLE.

WTC 2

WTC 1

78TH 84TH FLOORS

94TH 98TH FLOORS

THE WTC LACKED ANY PLAN FOR EVACUATION OF THE UPPER FLOORS IN THE EVENT ALL STAIRWELLS WERE IMPASSABLE.

NO DECISION HAS BEEN CRITIZED MORE THAN THAT OF BUILDING PERSONNEL NOT TO EVACUATE THE SOUTH TOWER AFTER THE NORTH WAS HIT.

LESS UNDERSTANDABLE TO THE COMMISSION WAS THE INSTRUCTION TO SOME CIVILIANS WHO HAD REACHED THE LOBBY TO RETURN TO THEIR OFFICES!

NYPD 911 OPERATORS AND FDNY DISPATCH WERE NOT ADEQUATELY INTEGRATED AND GAVE OUT WRONG DIRECTIONS.

ONE LESSON IS THE NEED TO INTEGRATE THEM INTO THE RESPONSE SYSTEM AND INVOLVE THEM IN PROVIDING UP-TO-DATE ASSISTANCE AND INFORMATION.

LADDER 2 FIRE

SORRY, THIS IS RESERVED FOR FIRE TRUCKS ONLY.

INDIVIDUALS SHOULD KNOW THE EXACT LOCATION OF EVERY STAIRWELL AND HAVE ACCESS AT ALL TIMES TO FLASHLIGHTS.

THOUGH MAYOR GIULIANI'S EMERGENCY DIRECTIVE OF JULY 2001 WAS FOLLOWED TO SOME DEGREE ...

...IT IS CLEAR THAT THE RESPONSE LACKED THE KIND OF INTEGRATED COMMUNICATION AND UNIFIED COMMAND CONTEMPLATED IN THE DIRECTIVE.

FOR A UNIFIED INCIDENT MANAGEMENT SYSTEM TO SUCCEED, EACH PARTICIPANT MUST HAVE CONTROL AND COMMAND OF ITS OWN UNITS AND ADEQUATE INTERNAL COMMUNICATIONS.

THIS WAS NOT ALWAYS THE CASE AT WTC ON 9/11.

AN EXAMPLE: THE FDNY PROVED INCAPABLE OF COORDINATING THE UNITS DISPATCHED TO DIFFERENT POINTS WITHIN THE 16-ACRE COMPLEX. TO ITS CREDIT, THE FDNY HAS ADDRESSED THESE PROBLEMS IN THE LAST THREE YEARS.

WE'RE BEING WASTED HERE AT THE MARRIOTT.

THE PORT AUTHORITY RESPONSE WAS HAMPERED BY LACK OF STANDARD OPERATING PROCEDURES AND APPROPRIATE RADIOS.

I CAN'T HEAR A WORD YOU'RE SAYING!

THE NYPD EXPERIENCED FEWER COMMAND AND COMMUNICATIONS ISSUES.

I CAN HEAR YOU, SIR. THERE ARE FIFTEEN OF US IN THE LOBBY.

ITS MISSION—— CROWD CONTROL—— WAS A FAMILIAR ONE.

THERE WAS A LACK OF COMPREHENSIVE COORDINATION AMONG FDNY, NYPD, AND PAPD PERSONNEL. INFORMATION WAS NOT SHARED.

FINALLY, WE'RE GETTING TOGETHER.

THE EMERGENCY RESPONSE PLAN ADOPTED BY NYC IN MAY 2004 FALLS SHORT OF AN OPTIMAL RESPONSE, WHICH REQUIRES CLEAR COMMAND AND CONTROL, COMMON TRAINING, AND THE TRUST THIS CREATES.

WE'VE GOTTEN WORD, SIR. WE'RE MOVING THEM ALONG.

THE LESSON OF 9/11 FOR CIVILIANS AND FIRST RESPONDERS CAN BE STATED SIMPLY: IN THE NEW AGE OF TERRORISM, THEY ARE THE PRIMARY TARGETS. THE LOSSES THAT DAY DEMONSTRATED THE GRAVITY OF THE THREAT AND THE NEED TO PREPARE OURSELVES. WE MUST PLAN FOR THE NEXT ATTACK. THIS IS PERHAPS THE BEST WAY TO HONOR THE MEMORIES OF THOSE WE LOST THAT DAY.

THE FDNY WAS FAR LESS SUCCESSFUL IN ALL THREE CATEGORIES.

RADIO COMMUNICATION WAS AN IMPORTANT FACTOR FOR ALL. THE NYPD WAS MOST SUCCESSFUL BECAUSE OF THE STRENGTH OF ITS RADIOS, THE SMALLER NUMBER OF RADIOS USED, AND THE USE OF THE CORRECT CHANNEL BY ALL.

Chapter 10: WARTIME

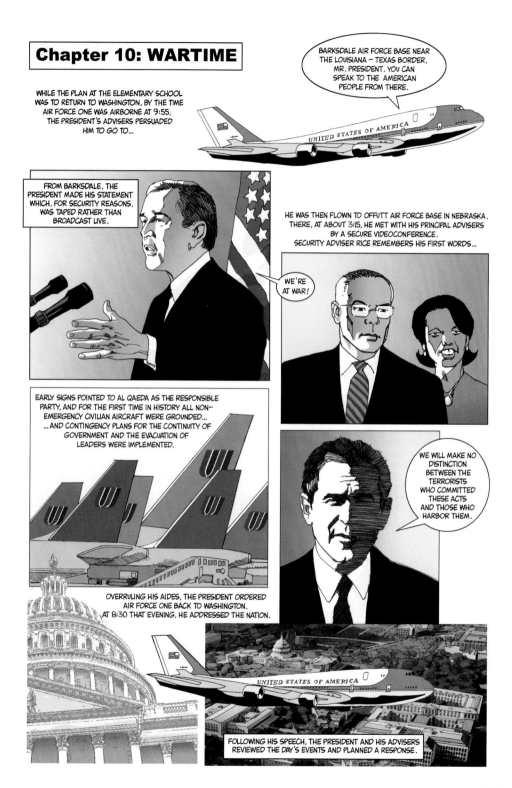

BARKSDALE AIR FORCE BASE NEAR THE LOUISIANA – TEXAS BORDER, MR. PRESIDENT. YOU CAN SPEAK TO THE AMERICAN PEOPLE FROM THERE.

WHILE THE PLAN AT THE ELEMENTARY SCHOOL WAS TO RETURN TO WASHINGTON, BY THE TIME AIR FORCE ONE WAS AIRBORNE AT 9:55, THE PRESIDENT'S ADVISERS PERSUADED HIM TO GO TO...

FROM BARKSDALE, THE PRESIDENT MADE HIS STATEMENT WHICH, FOR SECURITY REASONS, WAS TAPED RATHER THAN BROADCAST LIVE.

HE WAS THEN FLOWN TO OFFUTT AIR FORCE BASE IN NEBRASKA. THERE, AT ABOUT 3:15, HE MET WITH HIS PRINCIPAL ADVISERS BY A SECURE VIDEOCONFERENCE. SECURITY ADVISER RICE REMEMBERS HIS FIRST WORDS...

WE'RE AT WAR!

EARLY SIGNS POINTED TO AL QAEDA AS THE RESPONSIBLE PARTY, AND FOR THE FIRST TIME IN HISTORY ALL NON–EMERGENCY CIVILIAN AIRCRAFT WERE GROUNDED...
...AND CONTINGENCY PLANS FOR THE CONTINUITY OF GOVERNMENT AND THE EVACUATION OF LEADERS WERE IMPLEMENTED.

WE WILL MAKE NO DISTINCTION BETWEEN THE TERRORISTS WHO COMMITTED THESE ACTS AND THOSE WHO HARBOR THEM.

OVERRULING HIS AIDES, THE PRESIDENT ORDERED AIR FORCE ONE BACK TO WASHINGTON. AT 8:30 THAT EVENING, HE ADDRESSED THE NATION.

FOLLOWING HIS SPEECH, THE PRESIDENT AND HIS ADVISERS REVIEWED THE DAY'S EVENTS AND PLANNED A RESPONSE.

Immediate Responses at Home
FINDINGS OF THE COMMISSIONERS

TO HELP VICTIMS AND STANCH THE LOSSES TO THE AMERICAN ECONOMY, THE FEDERAL GOVERNMENT IMMEDIATELY ORGANIZED FEDERAL ASSISTANCE AND A FEDERAL COMPENSATION FUND.

ON SEPTEMBER 13, $20 BILLION WAS PROMISED TO NEW YORK CITY, IN ADDITION TO $20 BILLION FOR THE COUNTRY AS A WHOLE.

CIVIL AVIATION WAS RESTORED ON SEPTEMBER 13 AND THE FINANCIAL MARKETS WERE OPENED ON SEPTEMBER 17.

BORDER AND PORT SECURITY WERE RETURNED TO NORMAL OPERATION AND LEGISLATIVE PROPOSALS WERE EVALUATED TO BAIL OUT THE AIRLINE INDUSTRY.

ALL THIS UNDERSCORED THE ABSENCE OF AN EFFECTIVE GOVERNMENT AGENCY DEVOTED TO ASSESSING VULNERABILITIES AND HANDLING PROBLEMS OF PROTECTION AND PREPAREDNESS.

THE COMMISSION'S OWN INDEPENDENT REVIEW OF THE SAUDI NATIONALS INVOLVED CONFIRMS THAT NO ONE WITH KNOWN LINKS TO TERRORISM DEPARTED ON THESE CHARTER FLIGHTS.

BEGINNING ON SEPTEMBER 11, IMMIGRATION AND NATURALIZATION SERVICE AGENTS WORKING WITH THE FBI BEGAN ARRESTING INDIVIDUALS FOR IMMIGRATION VIOLATIONS.
768 ALIENS WERE ARRESTED AND SOME, SUCH AS ZACARIAS MOUSSAOUI, WERE IN CUSTODY BEFORE 9/11.

NO EVIDENCE WAS FOUND THAT ANY SAUDI NATIONALS FLED AMERICA BEFORE SEPTEMBER 13, EVERY FLIGHT OCCURRED AFTER THE NATIONAL AIRSPACE WAS REOPENED.

BY SEPTEMBER 14, VICE PRESIDENT CHENEY RECOMMENDED A NEW WHITE HOUSE ENTITY TO COORDINATE ALL RELEVANT AGENCIES INTO A HOMELAND SECURITY COUNCIL.
ON SEPTEMBER 20, THE PRESIDENT NAMED PENNSYLVANIA GOVERNOR TOM RIDGE AS ITS FIRST HOMELAND SECURITY ADVISER.

THE GOVERNMENT'S ABILITY TO COLLECT INTELLIGENCE INSIDE THE U.S. AND THE SHARING OF INFORMATION BETWEEN AGENCIES WERE NOT PRIORITIES BEFORE 9/11.
THE ATTACKS CHANGED EVERYTHING.

Planning for War

BY LATE EVENING SEPTEMBER 11, PRESIDENT BUSH CHAIRED A MEETING OF TOP ADVISERS HE LATER WOULD CALL HIS "WAR COUNCIL."

THE PRESIDENT TASKED HIS ADVISERS TO ELIMINATE "TERRORISM AS A THREAT TO OUR WAY OF LIFE."

THIS GROUP INCLUDED VICE PRESIDENT CHENEY, SECRETARY OF STATE POWELL, DEFENSE SECRETARY RUMSFELD, GENERALS SHELTON AND MYERS, DCI TENET, ATTORNEY GENERAL ASHCROFT, AND FBI DIRECTOR MUELLER.

THE PRESIDENT SAID IT WAS TIME FOR SELF-DEFENSE AND THAT THE U.S. WOULD PUNISH NOT JUST THE PERPETRATORS OF THE ATTACKS, BUT ALSO THOSE WHO HARBORED THEM.

SECRETARY POWELL SAID THE U.S. HAD TO MAKE IT CLEAR TO PAKISTAN, AFGHANISTAN, AND THE ARAB STATES THAT THE TIME TO ACT WAS NOW. WE NEEDED TO BUILD A COALITION.

SECRETARY RUMSFELD URGED THE PRESIDENT AND THE PRINCIPALS TO THINK BROADLY ABOUT WHO MIGHT HAVE HARBORED THE ATTACKERS, INCLUDING IRAQ, AFGHANISTAN, LIBYA, SUDAN, AND IRAN.

GENERAL HUGH SHELTON

GENERAL RICHARD MYERS

CIA DIRECTOR GEORGE TENET

U.S. ATTORNEY GENERAL JOHN ASHCROFT

FBI DIRECTOR ROBERT MUELLER

ON SEPTEMBER 13, DEPUTY SECRETARY OF STATE RICHARD ARMITAGE MET WITH TWO TOP PAKISTANI OFFICIALS AND INFORMED THEM THAT THE U.S. HAD A SERIES OF REQUESTS, INCLUDING...

(1) END ALL LOGISTICAL SUPPORT FOR AL QAEDA AND BIN LADIN AND GIVE THE U.S. OVERFLIGHT AND LANDING RIGHTS.
(2) PROVIDE THE U.S. WITH INTELLIGENCE INFORMATION AND CUT OFF ALL SHIPMENTS OF FUEL TO THE TALIBAN.
(3) STOP RECRUITS FROM GOING TO AFGHANISTAN, AND IF THE TALIBAN CONTINUES TO HARBOR BIN LADIN AND AL QAEDA, BREAK RELATIONS WITH ITS GOVERNMENT.
PAKISTAN AGREED WITH EVERY REQUEST.

OVER THE WEEKEND OF SEPTEMBER 15-16, THE PRESIDENT CONVENED HIS WAR COUNCIL AT CAMP DAVID.

JOINT CHIEFS CHAIRMAN GENERAL SHELTON BRIEFED THE PRINCIPALS ON THE PRELIMINARY MILITARY CAMPAIGN AND THE POSSIBLE USE OF GROUND FORCES.

CIA HEAD TENET DESCRIBED A PLAN FOR COLLECTING INTELLIGENCE AND MOUNTING COVERT ACTION IN AFGHANISTAN.

PRESIDENT BUSH DISCUSSED WITH RICE THE DIRECTIVES TO GET ALL PLANS IN MOTION. ON THE MORNING OF 9/17, BUSH STATED...

Afghanistan

Kabul

..."THE PURPOSE OF THIS MEETING IS TO ASSIGN TASKS FOR THE FIRST WAVE OF THE WAR AGAINST TERRORISM. IT STARTS TODAY."

THE PRESIDENT CHARGED ASHCROFT, MUELLER, AND TENET WITH DEVELOPING A PLAN FOR HOMELAND DEFENSE.

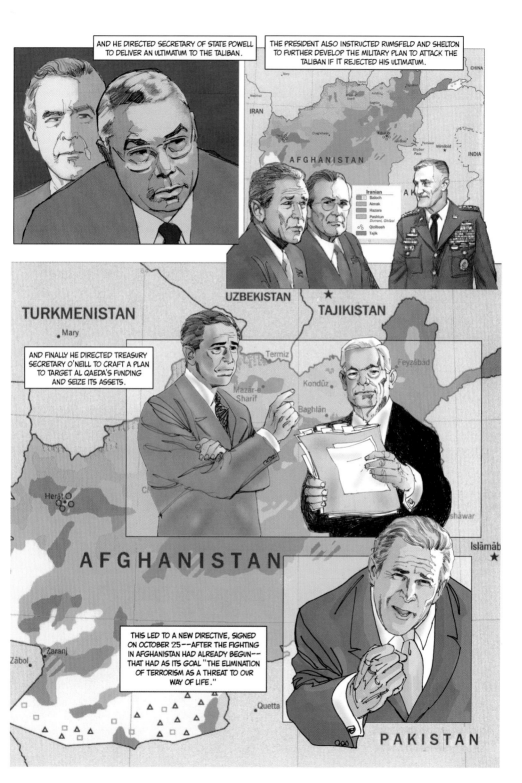

AND HE DIRECTED SECRETARY OF STATE POWELL TO DELIVER AN ULTIMATUM TO THE TALIBAN.

THE PRESIDENT ALSO INSTRUCTED RUMSFELD AND SHELTON TO FURTHER DEVELOP THE MILITARY PLAN TO ATTACK THE TALIBAN IF IT REJECTED HIS ULTIMATUM.

AND FINALLY HE DIRECTED TREASURY SECRETARY O'NEILL TO CRAFT A PLAN TO TARGET AL QAEDA'S FUNDING AND SEIZE ITS ASSETS.

THIS LED TO A NEW DIRECTIVE, SIGNED ON OCTOBER 25--AFTER THE FIGHTING IN AFGHANISTAN HAD ALREADY BEGUN--THAT HAD AS ITS GOAL "THE ELIMINATION OF TERRORISM AS A THREAT TO OUR WAY OF LIFE."

"Phase Two" and the Question of Iraq

PRESIDENT BUSH HAD WONDERED IMMEDIATELY AFTER THE ATTACK WHETHER SADDAM HUSSEIN'S REGIME HAD A HAND IN IT...

RICHARD CLARKE HAS WRITTEN THAT ON THE EVENING OF SEPTEMBER 12, THE PRESIDENT TOLD HIM...

SEE IF SADDAM DID THIS. SEE IF HE'S LINKED IN ANY WAY.

RESPONDING TO A PRESIDENTIAL TASKING, CLARKE SENT A MEMO TO RICE ON SEPTEMBER 18...

...TITLED "SURVEY OF INTELLIGENCE INFORMATION ON ANY IRAQ INVOLVEMENT IN THE SEPTEMBER 11 ATTACKS," IT FOUND ONLY SOME ANECDOTAL EVIDENCE LINKING IRAQ TO AL QAEDA... ZALMAY KHALILZAD, OF RICE'S STAFF, CONCURRED... THERE IS "NO COMPELLING CASE" THAT IRAQ EITHER PLANNED OR PERPETRATED THE ATTACKS. THE MEMO ADDED THAT BIN LADIN RESENTED THE SECULARISM OF HUSSEIN'S REGIME.

SECRETARY POWELL RECALLED THAT DEPUTY SECRETARY OF DEFENSE PAUL WOLFOWITZ ARGUED THAT IRAQ WAS THE SOURCE OF THE TERRORIST PROBLEM AND SHOULD BE ATTACKED, THOUGH HE WAS UNABLE TO JUSTIFY THAT BELIEF.

PAUL WAS ALWAYS OF THE VIEW THAT IRAQ WAS A PROBLEM THAT HAD TO BE DEALT WITH.

AND HE SAW THIS AS ONE WAY OF USING THIS EVENT AS A WAY TO DEAL WITH THE IRAQ PROBLEM.

ON SEPTEMBER 20, THE PRESIDENT MET WITH BRITISH PRIME MINISTER TONY BLAIR AND DISCUSSED THE GLOBAL CONFLICT AHEAD. ASKED ABOUT IRAQ, THE PRESIDENT SAID...

IRAQ IS NOT THE IMMEDIATE PROBLEM. SOME MEMBERS OF THE ADMINISTRATION HAVE EXPRESSED A DIFFERENT VIEW, BUT I'M THE ONE RESPONSIBLE FOR MAKING DECISIONS.

ON THURSDAY, SEPTEMBER 20, PRESIDENT BUSH ADDRESSED A JOINT SESSION OF CONGRESS.

TONIGHT WE ARE A COUNTRY AWAKENED TO DANGER.

PRESIDENT BUSH APPROVED MILITARY PLANS TO ATTACK AFGHANISTAN IN MEETINGS WITH GENERAL FRANKS AND OTHER ADVISERS ON SEPTEMBER 21 AND OCTOBER 2.

THE TALIBAN MUST ACT, AND ACT IMMEDIATELY. THEY WILL HAND OVER THE TERRORISTS, OR THEY WILL SHARE THEIR FATE.

THIS IS CIVILIZATION'S FIGHT. WE ASK EVERY NATION TO JOIN US.

ORIGINALLY TITLED "INFINITE JUSTICE," THE OPERATION'S CODE NAME WAS CHANGED TO "ENDURING FREEDOM."

IN PHASE ONE, THE U.S. AND ITS ALLIES MOVED FORCES INTO THE REGION AND ARRANGED TO OPERATE FROM OR OVER NEIGHBORING COUNTRIES, SUCH AS UZBEKISTAN AND PAKISTAN.

THIS OCCURRED IN THE WEEKS FOLLOWING 9/11, AIDED BY OVERWHELMING SYMPATHY FOR THE U.S.

IN PHASE TWO, AIR STRIKES AND SPECIAL OPERATIONS HIT KEY AL QAEDA AND TALIBAN TARGETS.

THESE BEGAN ON OCTOBER 7.

IN PHASE THREE, THE U.S. USED ALL ELEMENTS OF NATIONAL POWER, INCLUDING GROUND TROOPS, TO TOPPLE THE REGIME AND ELIMINATE AL QAEDA'S SANCTUARY IN AFGHANISTAN.
BY EARLY DECEMBER, ALL MAJOR CITIES HAD FALLEN TO COALITION FORCES COMPOSED OF U.S. AND ALLIED TROOPS.

ON DECEMBER 22, HAMID KARZAI, A PASHTUN LEADER FROM KANDAHAR, WAS INSTALLED AS CHAIRMAN OF THE NATION'S INTERIM ADMINISTRATION.

AFGHANISTAN HAD BEEN LIBERATED FROM THE RULE OF THE TALIBAN.

WITHIN ABOUT TWO MONTHS OF THE START OF OPERATIONS, THE TALIBAN REGIME WAS DESTROYED AND AL QAEDA WAS DISRUPTED.

THOUGH A QUARTER OF THE ENEMY'S LEADERS HAD BEEN KILLED OR CAPTURED, BIN LADIN AND ZAWAHIRI WERE STILL BELIEVED TO BE AT LARGE.

Chapter 11: FORESIGHT--AND HINDSIGHT

THE COMMISSION HAS TRIED TO REMEMBER THAT THEY WRITE WITH THE
BENEFIT AND THE HANDICAP OF HINDSIGHT.
WITH THAT CAUTION IN MIND, THEY ASKED THEMSELVES BEFORE THEY
JUDGED OTHERS WHETHER THE INSIGHTS THAT SEEM APPARENT NOW
WOULD REALLY HAVE BEEN MEANINGFUL AT THE TIME.
THE COMMISSION BELIEVES THE 9/11 ATTACKS REVEALED FOUR KINDS OF
FAILURE: IN IMAGINATION, IN POLICY, IN CAPABILITIES, AND IN MANAGEMENT.

Imagination

AMERICA HAD SUFFERED SURPRISE ATTACKS BEFORE 9/11. PEARL HARBOR IS A WELL-KNOWN CASE. THE 1950 CHINESE ATTACK IN KOREA IS ANOTHER.

BUT THESE WERE ATTACKS BY MAJOR POWERS.

WHILE BY NO MEANS AS THREATENING AS JAPAN'S ACT OF WAR, THE 9/11 ATTACK WAS IN SOME WAYS MORE DEVASTATING.

IT WAS CARRIED OUT BY A TINY GROUP OF PEOPLE WITH TRIVIAL RESOURCES OPERATING FROM ONE OF THE POOREST, LEAST INDUSTRIAL OF ALL NATIONS.

TO AMERICANS, AFGHANISTAN SEEMED VERY FAR AWAY. TO AL QAEDA, AMERICA SEEMED VERY CLOSE.

IN A SENSE, THEY WERE MORE GLOBALIZED THAN WE WERE.

WHILE WE NOW KNOW AL QAEDA WAS FORMED IN 1988, AT THE END OF THE SOVIET OCCUPATION OF AFGHANISTAN...

THE INTELLIGENCE COMMUNITY DID NOT DESCRIBE THIS ORGANIZATION, AT LEAST IN DOCUMENTS THE COMMISSION HAS SEEN, UNTIL 1999.

...THOUGH IN 1996–1997 THEY HAD LEARNED OF AL QAEDA'S INVOLVEMENT IN THE 1992 ATTACK ON A YEMENI HOTEL QUARTERING U.S. PERSONNEL, THE 1993 SHOOTDOWN OF ARMY BLACK HAWK HELICOPTERS IN SOMALIA...

...AND QUITE POSSIBLY THE 1995 RIYADH BOMBING OF AN AMERICAN MISSION TO THE SAUDI NATIONAL GUARD.

GIVEN THE CHARACTER AND PACE OF CLINTON'S AND BUSH'S POLICY EFFORTS, THE COMMISSION BELIEVES THEY DID NOT FULLY UNDERSTAND HOW MANY PEOPLE AL QAEDA MIGHT KILL AND HOW SOON IT MIGHT DO IT.

IT IS CRUCIAL TO FIND A WAY OF ROUTINIZING, EVEN BUREAUCRATIZING, THE EXERCISE OF IMAGINATION.

WITH THE IMPORTANT EXCEPTION OF ANALYSIS OF AL QAEDA EFFORTS IN CHEMICAL, RADIOLOGICAL, AND NUCLEAR WEAPONS, THE COMMISSION DID NOT FIND EVIDENCE THAT THE METHODS TO AVOID SURPRISE ATTACK THAT HAD BEEN LABORIOUSLY DEVELOPED WERE REGULARLY APPLIED.
CONSIDERING WHAT WAS **NOT** DONE SUGGESTS POSSIBLE WAYS TO INSTITUTIONALIZE IMAGINATION.

THE COUNTERTERRORIST CENTER (CTC) DID NOT ANALYZE HOW AN AIRCRAFT, HIJACKED OR EXPLOSIVES-LADEN, MIGHT BE USED AS A WEAPON, EVEN THOUGH SUICIDE TERRORISM HAD BECOME A PRINCIPAL TACTIC OF MIDDLE EASTERN TERRORISTS.
IF IT HAD DONE SO, THE COMMISSION BELIEVES IT MIGHT HAVE SPOTLIGHTED A CRITICAL RESTRAINT FOR THE TERRORISTS -- FINDING A SUICIDE OPERATIVE ABLE TO FLY A LARGE JET AIRCRAFT.

THE CTC DID NOT DEVELOP A SET OF TELLTALE INDICATORS FOR THIS METHOD OF ATTACK.

109

THERE ARE BIGGER FISH TO FRY THAN THIS AL QAEDA GANG OF THUGS.

BUT BECAUSE THE PRESIDENT WAS PREPARING FOR POSSIBLE WAR IN SERBIA, HAD AUTHORIZED MAJOR AIR STRIKES AGAINST IRAQ, AND FACED IMPEACHMENT PROCEEDINGS AT HOME, HIS WHITE HOUSE COULD NOT DO MUCH.

THE BEST TIME FOR MAJOR ACTION AGAINST AL QAEDA AND ITS SANCTUARY CAME IN THE LATE 1990s AFTER THE CLINTON ADMINISTRATION LEARNED OF THE GROUP'S ROLE IN SEVERAL BOMBINGS AND ATTACKS.

BUT LESSER FORMS OF INTERVENTION COULD HAVE BEEN CONSIDERED. ONE WOULD HAVE BEEN THE DEPLOYMENT OF U. S. MILITARY OR INTELLIGENCE PERSONNEL OR A SPECIAL STRIKE FORCE IN AFGHANISTAN.

BEFORE 9/11, THE DEPARTMENT OF DEFENSE WAS NOT GIVEN THE MISSION OF ENDING AL QAEDA'S SANCTUARY IN AFGHANISTAN, AND BOTH THE CLINTON AND BUSH ADMINISTRATIONS REGARDED A FULL U. S. INVASION OF THAT COUNTRY AS INCONCEIVABLE.

THE POSSIBILITY WAS NEVER THE SUBJECT OF FORMAL INTERAGENCY DELIBERATION.

ANOTHER POSSIBILITY WAS TO ISSUE A BLUNT ULTIMATUM TO THE TALIBAN BACKED BY A READINESS TO LAUNCH AN INDEFINITE AIR CAMPAIGN AND POSSIBLY TIP THE BALANCE IN AFGHANISTAN'S ONGOING CIVIL WAR.

Capabilities

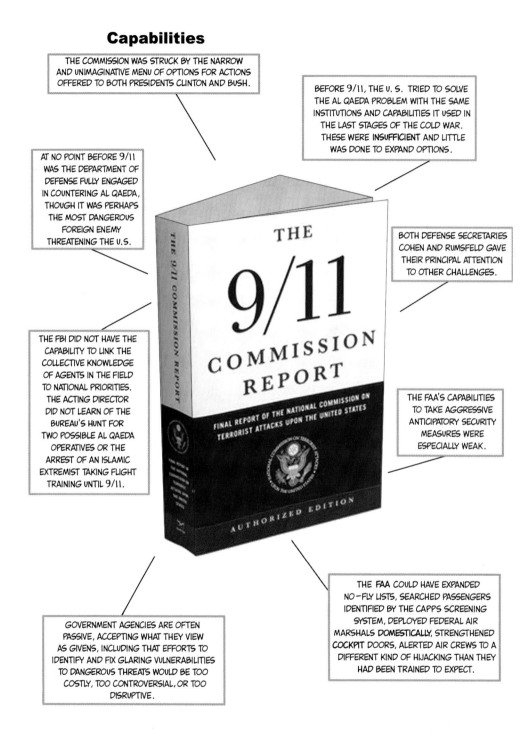

THE COMMISSION WAS STRUCK BY THE NARROW AND UNIMAGINATIVE MENU OF OPTIONS FOR ACTIONS OFFERED TO BOTH PRESIDENTS CLINTON AND BUSH.

BEFORE 9/11, THE U. S. TRIED TO SOLVE THE AL QAEDA PROBLEM WITH THE SAME INSTITUTIONS AND CAPABILITIES IT USED IN THE LAST STAGES OF THE COLD WAR. THESE WERE INSUFFICIENT AND LITTLE WAS DONE TO EXPAND OPTIONS.

AT NO POINT BEFORE 9/11 WAS THE DEPARTMENT OF DEFENSE FULLY ENGAGED IN COUNTERING AL QAEDA, THOUGH IT WAS PERHAPS THE MOST DANGEROUS FOREIGN ENEMY THREATENING THE U.S.

BOTH DEFENSE SECRETARIES COHEN AND RUMSFELD GAVE THEIR PRINCIPAL ATTENTION TO OTHER CHALLENGES.

THE FBI DID NOT HAVE THE CAPABILITY TO LINK THE COLLECTIVE KNOWLEDGE OF AGENTS IN THE FIELD TO NATIONAL PRIORITIES. THE ACTING DIRECTOR DID NOT LEARN OF THE BUREAU'S HUNT FOR TWO POSSIBLE AL QAEDA OPERATIVES OR THE ARREST OF AN ISLAMIC EXTREMIST TAKING FLIGHT TRAINING UNTIL 9/11.

THE FAA'S CAPABILITIES TO TAKE AGGRESSIVE ANTICIPATORY SECURITY MEASURES WERE ESPECIALLY WEAK.

GOVERNMENT AGENCIES ARE OFTEN PASSIVE, ACCEPTING WHAT THEY VIEW AS GIVENS, INCLUDING THAT EFFORTS TO IDENTIFY AND FIX GLARING VULNERABILITIES TO DANGEROUS THREATS WOULD BE TOO COSTLY, TOO CONTROVERSIAL, OR TOO DISRUPTIVE.

THE FAA COULD HAVE EXPANDED NO-FLY LISTS, SEARCHED PASSENGERS IDENTIFIED BY THE CAPPS SCREENING SYSTEM, DEPLOYED FEDERAL AIR MARSHALS DOMESTICALLY, STRENGTHENED COCKPIT DOORS, ALERTED AIR CREWS TO A DIFFERENT KIND OF HIJACKING THAN THEY HAD BEEN TRAINED TO EXPECT.

THE 9/11 COMMISSION REPORT

THE
9/11
COMMISSION
REPORT

FINAL REPORT OF THE NATIONAL COMMISSION ON TERRORIST ATTACKS UPON THE UNITED STATES

AUTHORIZED EDITION

Management

AS WAS POINTED OUT EARLIER, INFORMATION WAS NOT SHARED, ANALYSIS WAS NOT POOLED, AND EFFECTIVE OPERATIONS WERE NOT LAUNCHED. WHAT WAS MISSING WAS **AN AGENCY THAT** MADE SURE THE VARIOUS AGENCIES WORKED AS A TEAM.

SEVERAL CASES **HANDLED IN** 2000 AND THROUGH AUGUST 2001 REVEAL THE LACK OF SHARING FROM AGENCY TO AGENCY.

AND THUS OPPORTUNITIES TO STOP TERRORISTS WERE LOST.

THERE WAS ONE PERIOD, HOWEVER, IN WHICH **THE** GOVERNMENT AS A WHOLE SEEMED TO BE ACTING IN CONCERT TO DEAL WITH TERRORISM.

113

Chapter 12: WHAT TO DO? A GLOBAL STRATEGY

Reflecting on a Generational Challenge

THREE YEARS AFTER 9/11, COUNTERTERRORISM HAS BECOME THE TOP NATIONAL SECURITY PRIORITY FOR THE UNITED STATES.
FEDERAL SPENDING ON DEFENSE (INCLUDING EXPENDITURES FOR IRAN AND AFGHANISTAN), HOMELAND SECURITY, AND INTERNATIONAL AFFAIRS HAS RISEN MORE THAN 50%...

FROM $354 BILLION TO ABOUT $547 BILLION.

WE ARE NOW AT ORANGE ALERT.

THE U.S. SHOULD CONSIDER WHAT TO DO AND HOW TO DO IT, ORGANIZING THE GOVERNMENT IN A DIFFERENT WAY.

IN THE PAST, TO BE DANGEROUS, AN ENEMY HAD TO MUSTER LARGE ARMIES...

NOW, AN ORGANIZATION LIKE AL QAEDA, HEADQUARTERED IN A COUNTRY WITH LITTLE ELECTRICITY OR TELEPHONES...

THE PRESENT DANGER OF ISLAMIST TERRORISM NEEDS A BROAD, POLITICAL–MILITARY STRATEGY THAT...

- ATTACKS TERRORISTS AND THEIR ORGANIZATIONS
- PREVENTS THE CONTINUED GROWTH OF ISLAMIST TERRORISM
- PROTECTS AGAINST AND PREPARES FOR TERRORIST ATTACKS

... CAN SCHEME TO WIELD WEAPONS OF UNPRECEDENTED DESTRUCTIVE POWER.

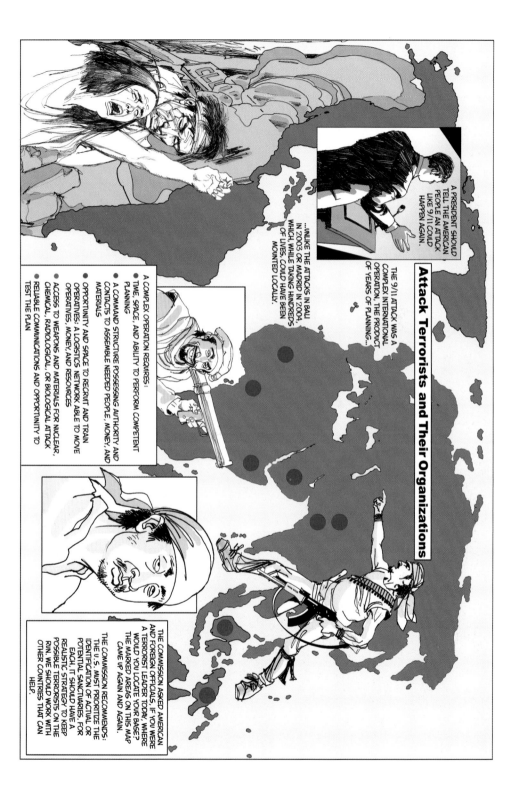

Attack Terrorists and Their Organizations

A PRESIDENT SHOULD TELL THE AMERICAN PEOPLE AN ATTACK LIKE 9/11 COULD HAPPEN AGAIN.

THE 9/11 ATTACK WAS A COMPLEX INTERNATIONAL OPERATION, THE PRODUCT OF YEARS OF PLANNING...

...UNLIKE THE ATTACKS IN BALI IN 2003 OR MADRID IN 2004, WHICH, WHILE TAKING HUNDREDS OF LIVES, COULD HAVE BEEN MOUNTED LOCALLY.

A COMPLEX OPERATION REQUIRES:

● TIME, SPACE, AND ABILITY TO PERFORM COMPETENT PLANNING

● A COMMAND STRUCTURE POSSESSING AUTHORITY AND CONTACTS TO ASSEMBLE NEEDED PEOPLE, MONEY, AND MATERIALS

● OPPORTUNITY AND SPACE TO RECRUIT AND TRAIN OPERATIVES; A LOGISTICS NETWORK ABLE TO MOVE OPERATIVES, MONEY, AND RESOURCES

● ACCESS TO WEAPONS AND MATERIALS FOR NUCLEAR, CHEMICAL, RADIOLOGICAL, OR BIOLOGICAL ATTACK

● RELIABLE COMMUNICATIONS AND OPPORTUNITY TO TEST THE PLAN

THE COMMISSION ASKED AMERICAN AND FOREIGN OFFICIALS, IF YOU WERE A TERRORIST LEADER TODAY, WHERE WOULD YOU LOCATE YOUR BASE? THE MARKED AREAS ON THIS MAP CAME UP AGAIN AND AGAIN.

THE COMMISSION RECOMMENDS: THE U.S. MUST PRIORITIZE THE IDENTIFICATION OF ACTUAL OR POTENTIAL SANCTUARIES. FOR EACH, IT SHOULD HAVE A REALISTIC STRATEGY TO KEEP POSSIBLE TERRORISTS ON THE RUN. WE SHOULD WORK WITH OTHER COUNTRIES THAT CAN HELP.

PAKISTAN'S ENDEMIC POVERTY, WIDESPREAD CORRUPTION, AND OFTEN INEFFECTIVE GOVERNMENT CREATE OPPORTUNITIES FOR ISLAMIST RECRUITMENT.

MILLIONS OF FAMILIES, ESPECIALLY THE POOR, SEND THEIR CHILDREN TO RELIGIOUS SCHOOLS, OR MADRASSAS. MANY OF THESE SCHOOLS HAVE BEEN USED AS INCUBATORS FOR VIOLENT EXTREMISM. IN KARACHI ALONE, THERE ARE 859 MADRASSAS TEACHING MORE THAN 200,000 YOUNGSTERS.

WITHIN THE COUNTRY'S BORDERS ARE 150 MILLION MUSLIMS, SCORES OF AL QAEDA TERRORISTS, MANY TALIBAN FIGHTERS, AND PERHAPS USAMA BIN LADIN.

PAKISTAN'S VAST UNPOLICED REGIONS MAKE IT ATTRACTIVE TO EXTREMISTS SEEKING REFUGE AND RECRUITS...

...AS WELL AS BASES OF OPERATIONS AGAINST COALITION FORCES IN AFGHANISTAN.

DESPITE THE CHECKERED PAST OF PAKISTANI PRESIDENT PERVEZ MUSHARRAF—— HE HELPED NURTURE THE TALIBAN, HE WON'T BARTER WITH THE NATION'S NUCLEAR TECHNOLOGY, HE HAS NOT MOVED TOWARD DEMOCRACY, BUT HE DID SUPPORT THE U. S. IN AFGHANISTAN——THE COMMISSION BELIEVES...

...THAT IF MUSHARRAF STANDS FOR ENLIGHTENED MODERATION, THE U.S. SHOULD MAKE THE LONG-TERM COMMITMENT TO PAKISTAN'S FUTURE AND SUPPORT THE GOVERNMENT IN ITS STRUGGLE AGAINST EXTREMISTS, MILITARILY AND IN EDUCATION.

THE TALIBAN REGIME IN AFGHANISTAN--THE INCUBATOR FOR AL QAEDA AND THE 9/11 ATTACKS--WAS TOPPLED BY THE U.S.-LED COALITION IN THE FALL OF 2001.

MORE THAN 10,000 AMERICAN SOLDIERS AS WELL AS A NATO-LED FORCE AND SOLDIERS FROM MUSLIM STATES ARE DEPLOYED THERE TODAY.

A CENTRAL GOVERNMENT HAS BEEN ESTABLISHED IN KABUL, WITH A DEMOCRATIC CONSTITUTION, NEW CURRENCY AND ARMY, AND A BRAVE AND COMMITTED PRESIDENT IN HAMID KARZAI.

THERE IS GREATER FREEDOM, WOMEN AND GIRLS ARE EMERGING FROM SUBJUGATION, AND THREE MILLION CHILDREN HAVE RETURNED TO SCHOOL.

BUT TALIBAN AND AL QAEDA FIGHTERS HAVE REGROUPED IN THE SOUTH, WARLORDS CONTROL MUCH OF THE COUNTRY, THE LAND IS AWASH IN WEAPONS...

...AND THE NARCOTICS TRADE IS AGAIN BOOMING.

THE COMMISSION BELIEVES THAT THE PRESIDENT AND CONGRESS DESERVE PRAISE FOR THEIR EFFORTS SO FAR. NOW THEY AND THE INTERNATIONAL COMMUNITY MUST MAKE A LONG-TERM COMMITMENT TO A SECURE AND STABLE AFGHANISTAN.

BUT THE U.S. PRESENCE IS OVERWHELMINGLY ORIENTED TOWARD MILITARY AND SECURITY WORK. THE STATE DEPARTMENT PRESENCE MUST BE GREATER AND THERE MUST BE MORE DONE TO RESTORE THE RULE OF LAW AND CONTAIN RAMPANT CRIME AND NARCOTICS TRAFFICKING.

THE WAHHABI SECT THAT FLOURISHES IN SAUDI ARABIA HAS FUNDED SCHOOLS THROUGHOUT THE ISLAMIC WORLD, MANY OF WHICH HAVE BEEN EXPLOITED BY EXTREMISTS TO PROPAGATE THEIR VIEWS.

U.S. LEADERS AND SAUDI RULERS HAVE LONG HAD FRIENDLY RELATIONS, ROOTED IN COMMON ANTI-SOVIETISM DURING THE COLD WAR, U.S. HOPES FOR AID IN THE OIL MARKET, AND SAUDI HOPES FOR PROTECTION AGAINST FOREIGN THREATS.

MANY AMERICANS, HOWEVER, ARE APPALLED BY SAUDI INTOLERANCE, ANTI-SEMITISM, AND ANTI-AMERICAN ARGUMENTS TAUGHT IN SCHOOLS AND MOSQUES.

THE COMMISSION RECOMMENDS THAT THE U.S.-SAUDI RELATIONSHIP BE CONFRONTED OPENLY. IT SHOULD INCLUDE A SAUDI COMMITMENT TO POLITICAL AND ECONOMIC REFORM, GREATER TOLERANCE AND CULTURAL RESPECT, AND A COMMITMENT TO FIGHT THE VIOLENT EXTREMISTS WHO FOMENT HATRED.

Prevent the Continued Growth of Islamist Terrorism

IN OCTOBER 2003, REFLECTING ON PROGRESS AFTER TWO YEARS OF WAGING THE WAR ON TERRORISM, SECRETARY RUMSFELD ASKED HIS ADVISERS...

ARE WE CAPTURING, KILLING, OR DETERRING AND DISSUADING MORE TERRORISTS EVERY DAY THAN THE MADRASSAS AND THE RADICAL CLERICS ARE RECRUITING, TRAINING, AND DEPLOYING AGAINST US?

THE COMMISSION BELIEVES THESE ARE THE RIGHT QUESTIONS. THEIR ANSWER IS THAT WE NEED SHORT-TERM ACTION ON A LONG-RANGE STRATEGY, ONE THAT INVIGORATES OUR FOREIGN POLICY WITH THE ATTENTION GIVEN THE MILITARY AND INTELLIGENCE PARTS OF THE CONFLICT.

DOES THE U.S. NEED TO FASHION A BROAD INTEGRATED PLAN TO STOP THE NEXT GENERATION OF TERRORISTS? THE U.S. IS PUTTING RELATIVELY LITTLE EFFORT INTO A LONG-RANGE PLAN.

EGYPT

SAUDI ARABIA

POLLS IN 2002 FOUND THAT AMONG FRIENDS, LIKE EGYPT AND SAUDI ARABIA, ONLY 15% AND 12% HAD A FAVORABLE OPINION OF THE U.S. IN 2003, NEGATIVE VIEWS OF THE U.S. AMONG MUSLIMS HAD SPREAD BEYOND THE MIDDLE EAST. FAVORABLE RATINGS HAD DROPPED FROM 61% TO 15% IN INDONESIA AND FROM 71% TO 38% AMONG NIGERIAN MUSLIMS.

The Commission Recommends:

WE SHOULD OFFER AN EXAMPLE OF MORAL LEADERSHIP COMMITTED TO TREAT PEOPLE HUMANELY, ABIDE BY THE RULE OF LAW, AND BE GENEROUS AND CARING TO OUR NEIGHBORS.
THE VISION OF THE FUTURE SHOULD STRESS LIFE OVER DEATH: INDIVIDUAL EDUCATIONAL AND ECONOMIC OPPORTUNITY.

NEITHER ISRAEL NOR THE NEW IRAQ WILL BE SAFER IF WORLDWIDE ISLAMIST TERRORISM GROWS.
WE NEED TO DEFEND OUR IDEALS ABROAD VIGOROUSLY.
WE SHOULD STRIVE TO REACH LARGE AUDIENCES ON SATELLITE TV AND RADIO.

THE U.S. SHOULD REBUILD THE SCHOLARSHIP, EXCHANGE, AND LIBRARY PROGRAMS THAT REACH OUT TO YOUNG PEOPLE.
THE COMMISSION RECOMMENDS THAT THE U.S. JOIN WITH OTHER NATIONS IN GENEROUSLY SUPPORTING A NEW INTERNATIONAL YOUTH OPPORTUNITY FUND.
THIS WOULD HELP IN BUILDING PRIMARY AND SECONDARY SCHOOLS IN MUSLIM STATES THAT COMMIT TO INVESTING THEIR OWN MONEY IN PUBLIC EDUCATION.
THE U.S. HAS BEEN SEEKING FREE-TRADE AGREEMENTS WITH MIDDLE EASTERN NATIONS MOST FIRMLY ON THE PATH TO REFORM.

THE COMMISSION RECOMMENDS A COMPREHENSIVE U.S. STRATEGY TO COUNTER TERRORISM. IT SHOULD INCLUDE ECONOMIC POLICIES THAT ENCOURAGE DEVELOPMENT, MORE OPEN SOCIETIES, AND OPPORTUNITIES FOR PEOPLE TO IMPROVE THEIR LIVES AND THEIR CHILDREN'S FUTURE.

THERE SHOULD ALSO BE A COMPREHENSIVE COALITION STRATEGY AGAINST ISLAMIST TERRORISM, INCLUDING A JOINT STRATEGY FOR TARGETING TERRORIST TRAVEL AND A COMMON STRATEGY FOR DEALING WITH THEIR PLACES OF SANCTUARY. ALLEGATIONS THAT THE U.S. ABUSED PRISONERS MAKE IT HARDER TO BUILD THE DIPLOMATIC, POLITICAL, AND MILITARY ALLIANCES THE GOVERNMENT WILL NEED.

THE COMMISSION RECOMMENDS THAT THE U.S. ENGAGE ITS FRIENDS TO DEVELOP A COMMON COALITION APPROACH TOWARD THE DETENTION AND HUMANE TREATMENT OF CAPTURED TERRORISTS.
NEW PRINCIPLES MIGHT DRAW UPON ARTICLE 3 OF THE GENEVA CONVENTION.

THE COMMISSION'S REPORT SHOWS THAT AL QAEDA TRIED TO MAKE WEAPONS OF MASS DESTRUCTION FOR AT LEAST TEN YEARS.

DCI TENET'S FEBRUARY 2004 WORLDWIDE THREAT ASSESSMENT TO CONGRESS POINTED OUT THAT BIN LADIN CONSIDERED ACQUIRING WMD A "RELIGIOUS OBLIGATION."

TENET WARNED THAT AL QAEDA "CONTINUES TO PURSUE ITS STRATEGIC GOAL OF OBTAINING A NUCLEAR CAPABILITY."

AN AMOUNT OF PLUTONIUM THE SIZE OF AN ORANGE COULD BE FASHIONED INTO A NUCLEAR DEVICE THAT COULD FIT INTO A VAN LIKE THE ONE IN THE 1993 WTC BOMBING... AND LEVEL LOWER MANHATTAN.

PREVENTING THE PROLIFERATION OF WEAPONS OF MASS DESTRUCTION WARRANTS A MAXIMUM EFFORT BY THE U.S. AND OTHER NATIONS.

ARAB CHARITIES AND

THE MAIN INSTRUMENT IS AN EXPANDED AND IMPROVED COOPERATIVE THREAT REDUCTION PROGRAM (ALSO KNOWN AS "NUNN-LUGAR").

VIGOROUS EFFORTS TO TRACK FINANCING MUST REMAIN FRONT AND CENTER IN U.S. COUNTERTERRORISM EFFORTS.

THE DEATH OR CAPTURE OF SEVERAL FACILITATORS HAS DECREASED THE MONEY AVAILABLE TO AL QAEDA AND PROVIDED A WINDFALL OF INTELLIGENCE THAT CAN BE USED TO CONTINUE THE CYCLE OF DISRUPTION.

HOWEVER, IF AL QAEDA IS REPLACED BY SMALL, DECENTRALIZED GROUPS, THESE METHODS MAY BE OUTDATED. IN ADDITION, SOME TERRORIST ORGANIZATIONS MAY NOW BE SELF-FUNDING, EITHER THROUGH LEGITIMATE EMPLOYMENT OR LOW-LEVEL CRIMINAL ACTIVITY.

Protect Against and Prepare for Terrorist Attacks

IN THE YEARS SINCE 9/11, AMERICANS HAVE BEEN BETTER PROTECTED AGAINST TERRORIST ATTACKS BECAUSE OF THE SHEER SCALE OF SPENDING, CERTAIN GOVERNMENT ACTIONS SUCH AS NEW PRECAUTIONS IN AIRCRAFT, PUBLICITY, AND AMERICAN VIGILANCE. SAFER, BUT NOT SAFE.

MORE THAN 500 MILLION PEOPLE ANNUALLY CROSS U.S. BORDERS AT LEGAL ENTRY POINTS, ABOUT 330 MILLION OF THEM NONCITIZENS. TERRORISTS USE EVASIVE METHODS, SUCH AS ALTERED AND COUNTERFEIT PASSPORTS AND VISAS THAT CAN SOMETIMES BE DETECTED.

PRIOR TO 9/11, IF THE U.S. HAD ANALYZED TERRORISTS' TRAVEL STRATEGIES, WE MIGHT HAVE PREVENTED MUCH DAMAGE.

THE COMMISSION FOUND THAT 15 OF THE 19 HIJACKERS WERE POTENTIALLY VULNERABLE TO INTERCEPTION BY BORDER AUTHORITIES.

THE U.S. SHOULD COMBINE TERRORIST TRAVEL INTELLIGENCE, OPERATIONS, AND LAW ENFORCEMENT TO INTERCEPT TERRORISTS, FIND THEIR TRAVEL FACILITATORS, AND CONTAIN THEIR MOBILITY.

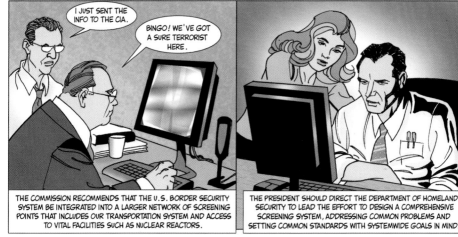

THE COMMISSION RECOMMENDS THAT THE U.S. BORDER SECURITY SYSTEM BE INTEGRATED INTO A LARGER NETWORK OF SCREENING POINTS THAT INCLUDES OUR TRANSPORTATION SYSTEM AND ACCESS TO VITAL FACILITIES SUCH AS NUCLEAR REACTORS.

THE PRESIDENT SHOULD DIRECT THE DEPARTMENT OF HOMELAND SECURITY TO LEAD THE EFFORT TO DESIGN A COMPREHENSIVE SCREENING SYSTEM, ADDRESSING COMMON PROBLEMS AND SETTING COMMON STANDARDS WITH SYSTEMWIDE GOALS IN MIND.

SINCE 9/11, THE U. S. HAS BUILT THE FIRST PHASE OF A BIOMETRIC SCREENING PROGRAM CALLED US VISIT, WHICH UTILIZES TWO IDENTIFIERS -- DIGITAL PHOTOS AND PRINTS OF TWO INDEX FINGERS -- FROM TRAVELERS.

SO FAR, ONLY VISITORS WHO ACQUIRE VISAS ARE COVERED, AND THE FULL SYSTEM MAY NOT BE INSTALLED BEFORE 2010, A TIMETABLE THAT MAY BE TOO SLOW.

THE COMMISSION RECOMMENDS THAT THE DEPARTMENT OF HOMELAND SECURITY COMPLETE AS QUICKLY AS POSSIBLE A BIOMETRIC ENTRY-EXIT SCREENING SYSTEM AND WORK WITH OTHER COUNTRIES TO ENSURE EFFECTIVE INSPECTION AT ALL AIRPORTS.

UH-OH. WE JUST RECEIVED WORD ON THIS CHAP FROM THE AMERICANS. HE'S DANGEROUS.

THE U.S. CANNOT MEET ITS OBLIGATIONS TO PREVENT THE ENTRY OF TERRORISTS WITHOUT A MAJOR EFFORT TO COLLABORATE WITH OTHER NATIONS.

WE CAN'T LET YOU THROUGH WITH THIS, SIR. IT'S NOT GENUINE.

THE FEDERAL GOVERNMENT SHOULD SET STANDARDS FOR THE ISSUANCE OF BIRTH CERTIFICATES AND SOURCES OF IDENTIFICATION -- LIKE DRIVER'S LICENSES. FRAUD IS NO LONGER JUST A PROBLEM OF THEFT.

DON'T WORRY, THEY DON'T CHECK THESE LOADS.

THE TRANSPORTATION SECURITY ADMINISTRATION, CREATED IN NOVEMBER 2001 AND NOW PART OF THE HOMELAND SECURITY DEPARTMENT, HELPED DEVELOP STRATEGIC PLANS TO PROTECT THE TRANSPORTATION SECTOR.

BUT MAJOR VULNERABILITIES STILL EXIST IN CARGO AND AVIATION SECURITY AND, PERHAPS MORE IMPORTANTLY, IN MARITIME AND SURFACE TRANSPORTATION.

Chapter 13: HOW TO DO IT? A DIFFERENT WAY OF ORGANIZING THE GOVERNMENT

IN THE 1940S AND 1950S, GOVERNMENT WAS RESTRUCTURED SO THAT IT COULD PROTECT THE COUNTRY. NOW, AFTER 9/11, TO DEAL WITH THIS DIFFERENT WORLD, THE COMMISSION RECOMMENDS FIVE SIGNIFICANT CHANGES IN THE ORGANIZATION OF GOVERNMENT.

UNIFYING STRATEGIC INTELLIGENCE AND OPERATIONAL PLANNING AGAINST ISLAMIST TERRORISTS ACROSS THE FOREIGN–DOMESTIC DIVIDE WITH A NATIONAL COUNTERTERRORISM CENTER.

UNIFYING THE INTELLIGENCE COMMUNITY WITH A NEW NATIONAL INTELLIGENCE DIRECTOR.

UNIFYING THE PARTICIPANTS IN THIS EFFORT AND THEIR KNOWLEDGE IN A NETWORK–BASED INFORMATION–SHARING SYSTEM.

UNIFYING AND STRENGTHENING CONGRESSIONAL OVERSIGHT TO IMPROVE QUALITY AND ACCOUNTABILITY.

STRENGTHENING THE FBI AND HOMELAND DEFENDERS.

Unity of Effort Across the Foreign-Domestic Divide

BEFORE 9/11, THE CIA WAS THE LEAD AGENCY CONFRONTING AL QAEDA. THE FBI PLAYED A SECONDARY ROLE. THE PARTICIPATION OF THE STATE AND DEFENSE DEPARTMENTS WAS MORE EPISODIC. TODAY THE U.S. GOVERNMENT CANNOT AFFORD SO MUCH DUPLICATION OF EFFORT. THERE ARE NOT ENOUGH EXPERIENCED EXPERTS TO GO AROUND.

SECRETARY RUMSFELD TOLD THE COMMISSION THAT TO ACHIEVE BETTER GOVERNMENT CAPABILITY, EACH OF THE ARMED FORCES HAD TO...

GIVE UP SOME OF THEIR TURF AND AUTHORITIES AND PREROGATIVES.

HE WONDERED IF IT MIGHT BE APPROPRIATE TO ASK AGENCIES TO...

TODAY THE EXECUTIVE BRANCH IS...

GIVE UP SOME OF THEIR EXISTING TURF AND AUTHORITY FOR A STRONGER, FASTER, MORE EFFICIENT GOVERNMENT-WIDE EFFORT.

STOVE-PIPED MUCH LIKE THE FOUR SERVICES WERE NEARLY TWENTY YEARS AGO.

PRIVATELY, OTHER KEY OFFICIALS MADE THE SAME POINT TO THE COMMISSION.

THE COMMISSION PROPOSES THE ESTABLISHMENT OF A NEW INSTITUTION, THE NATIONAL COUNTERTERRORISM CENTER (NCTC), A CIVILIAN-LED UNIFIED JOINT COMMAND FOR COUNTER-TERRORISM.
IT SHOULD COMBINE STRATEGIC INTELLIGENCE AND JOINT OPERATIONAL PLANNING AND BE STAFFED BY PERSONNEL FROM THE VARIOUS AGENCIES.

IT SHOULD PERFORM JOINT PLANNING, ASSIGNING RESPONSIBILITIES TO LEAD AGENCIES, SUCH AS STATE, CIA, FBI, DEFENSE, HOMELAND SECURITY, AND OTHERS.

IT SHOULD NOT BE A POLICY-MAKING BODY BUT SHOULD FOLLOW THE POLICY DIRECTION OF THE PRESIDENT AND THE NATIONAL SECURITY COUNCIL. THE HEAD OF THE NCTC SHOULD BE APPOINTED BY THE PRESIDENT AND BE EQUIVALENT TO A DEPUTY HEAD OF A CABINET DEPARTMENT.

SUCH A CENTER SHOULD BE DEVELOPED IN THE SAME SPIRIT THAT GUIDED THE MILITARY'S CREATION OF UNIFIED JOINT COMMANDS.

IT SHOULD LEAD STRATEGIC ANALYSIS, POOLING ALL-SOURCE INTELLIGENCE, FOREIGN AND DOMESTIC, ABOUT TRANSNATIONAL TERRORIST ORGANIZATIONS.

COUNTERING TRANSNATIONAL ISLAMIST TERRORISM WILL TEST WHETHER THE U.S. CAN FASHION MORE FLEXIBLE MANAGEMENT NEEDED TO DEAL WITH THE 21ST-CENTURY WORLD.

Unity of Effort in the Intelligence Community

THE COMMISSION BELIEVES THE INTELLIGENCE COMMUNITY NEEDS TO BE RECONSTRUCTED.
THE FOLLOWING ARE SOME OF THE PROBLEMS...

AND THIS IS WHAT WE PROPOSE.

NATIONAL INTELLIGENCE IS STILL ORGANIZED AROUND THE COLLECTION DISCIPLINES OF HOME AGENCIES, NOT THE JOINT MISSION. BY CONTRAST, IN ORGANIZING NATIONAL DEFENSE, THE GOLDWATER/NICHOLS LEGISLATION OF 1986 CREATED JOINT COMMANDS FOR OPERATIONS, AND ITS OPERATIONS BECAME MORE INTEGRATED.

THERE IS A LACK OF COMMON STANDARDS AND PRACTICES ACROSS THE FOREIGN-DOMESTIC DIVIDE.

WHO KNOWS WHO THEY'RE USING IN LEBANON AND WHAT IT'S WORTH.

THE INTELLIGENCE COMMUNITY SHOULD BE ABLE TO POOL ALL INFORMATION-- WHEREVER IT'S DONE.

DO WE CALL THE CIA ON THIS?

WE'RE NOT ALLOWED.

THERE IS A DIVIDED MANAGEMENT OF NATIONAL INTELLIGENCE CAPABILITIES.

THE AGENCIES WITHIN THE DEPARTMENT OF DEFENSE RELY HEAVILY ON INTELLIGENCE SYSTEMS-- SATELLITES IN PARTICULAR-- LEAVING THE DCI AND THE CIA LESS INFLUENTIAL.

IF ONLY WE WERE CONNECTED TO THEIR SATELLITE SYSTEM.

THE AGENCIES ARE MAINLY ORGANIZED AROUND WHAT THEY COLLECT OR THE WAY THEY COLLECT IT.

THE DCI MUST HAVE THE POWER TO REACH ACROSS AGENCIES AND REALLOCATE EFFORT.

THE DCI HAS TOO MANY JOBS, AND THE AGENCY'S RULES ARE TOO COMPLEX AND SECRET.

WITH ALL MY SUPPOSED POWERS, I CAN'T FIRE A PERFECT FOOL PUT INTO THE INTELLIGENCE COMMUNITY BY THE DEFENSE DEPARTMENT.

DON'T GET HIM STARTED ON THE FBI.

EVEN THE MOST BASIC INFORMATION ABOUT ALLOCATION OF FUNDS IS SHROUDED FROM PUBLIC VIEW.

THE COMMISSION RECOMMENDS THAT THE CURRENT POSITION OF DIRECTOR OF CENTRAL INTELLIGENCE BE REPLACED BY A NATIONAL INTELLIGENCE DIRECTOR. HE OR SHE WOULD OVERSEE NATIONAL INTELLIGENCE CENTERS ON SPECIFIC SUBJECTS OF INTEREST AND MANAGE THE INTELLIGENCE PROGRAM AND OVERSEE ITS AGENCIES. THE DUTIES AND THE OFFICES UNDER COMMAND WOULD BE AS FOLLOWS:

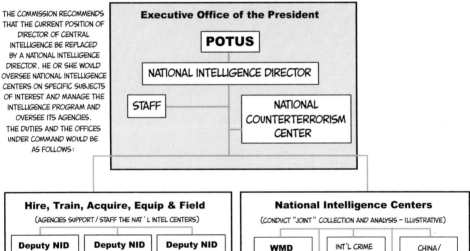

Executive Office of the President

POTUS

NATIONAL INTELLIGENCE DIRECTOR

STAFF

NATIONAL COUNTERTERRORISM CENTER

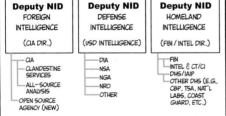

Hire, Train, Acquire, Equip & Field

(AGENCIES SUPPORT / STAFF THE NAT'L INTEL CENTERS)

Deputy NID
FOREIGN INTELLIGENCE
(CIA DIR.)
- CIA
- CLANDESTINE SERVICES
- ALL-SOURCE ANALYSIS
- OPEN SOURCE AGENCY (NEW)

Deputy NID
DEFENSE INTELLIGENCE
(USD INTELLIGENCE)
- DIA
- NSA
- NGA
- NRO
- OTHER

Deputy NID
HOMELAND INTELLIGENCE
(FBI / INTEL DIR.)
- FBI
- INTEL & CT/CI
- DHS/IAIP
- OTHER DHS (E.G., CBP, TSA, NAT'L LABS, COAST GUARD, ETC.)

National Intelligence Centers

(CONDUCT "JOINT" COLLECTION AND ANALYSIS - ILLUSTRATIVE)

WMD PROLIFERATION

INT'L CRIME & NARCOTICS

CHINA/ EAST ASIA

MIDDLE EAST

RUSSIA/ EURASIA

CAN YOU CONNECT THE DOTS?

AND THE PHRASE IN ARABIC IS?

good morning
can ...to the

THE COMMISSION RECOMMENDS THAT THE CIA DIRECTOR EMPHASIZE REBUILDING ITS ANALYTIC CAPABILITIES, BUILD A STRONGER LANGUAGE PROGRAM, RENEW EMPHASIS ON RECRUITING DIVERSITY SO AGENTS CAN BLEND MORE EASILY IN FOREIGN CITIES.

NOW *THIS* IS WHAT OUR DEPARTMENT SHOULD LOOK LIKE.

...INCLUDING PROPAGANDA AND NONMILITARY DISRUPTION.

THE COMMISSION RECOMMENDS THAT THE CIA RETAIN RESPONSIBILITY FOR CLANDESTINE AND COVERT OPERATIONS...

WE WOULD LIKE NO ONE TO SHOW UP FOR WORK TOMORROW.

LEAD RESPONSIBILITY FOR DIRECTING AND EXECUTING PARAMILITARY OPERATIONS, CLANDESTINE OR COVERT, SHOULD SHIFT TO THE DEFENSE DEPARTMENT. THERE IT SHOULD BE CONSOLIDATED WITH THE CAPABILITIES FOR TRAINING.

WE STORM THE CAVE AT 0500. YOU KNOW WHAT WE'RE AFTER, GENTLEMEN.

THE U.S. CANNOT AFFORD TO BUILD TWO SEPARATE CAPABILITIES FOR CARRYING OUT THOSE OPERATIONS.

TO COMBAT THE SECRECY AND COMPLEXITY OF CURRENT CONGRESSIONAL FUNDING, THE COMMISSION RECOMMENDS THAT THE OVER-ALL AMOUNTS OF MONEY APPROPRIATED FOR NATIONAL INTELLIGENCE NO LONGER BE KEPT SECRET.

WE DO, AFTER ALL, PROVIDE INFORMATION ON ALL MILITARY SPENDING.

UNITED STATES CONGRESS

THE SPECIFICS OF THE OPERATION WOULD REMAIN CLASSIFIED, WHICH WOULD STILL MAKE IT HARD FOR THE OUTSIDE WORLD TO JUDGE PRIORITIES.

128

Unity of Effort in Sharing Information

NOT ONLY DOES INTELLIGENCE WIN WARS, BUT THE BEST INTELLIGENCE ENABLES US TO PREVENT WARS FROM HAPPENING ALTOGETHER.

THE OTHER REFORMS WE HAVE SUGGESTED WILL NOT WORK IF CONGRESSIONAL OVERSIGHT DOES NOT CHANGE TOO.

WE HAVE CONSIDERED VARIOUS ALTERNATIVES- A JOINT COMMITTEE ON THE OLD MODEL OF THE JOINT COMMITTEE ON ATOMIC ENERGY IS ONE; A SINGLE COMMITTEE IN EACH HOUSE OF CONGRESS, COMBINING AUTHORIZING AND APPROPRIATING AUTHORITIES, IS ANOTHER.

MEMBERS SHOULD SERVE INDEFINITELY ON THE INTELLIGENCE COMMITTEES, WITHOUT SET TERMS, LETTING THEM ACCUMULATE EXPERTISE.

THE MAJORITY PARTY'S REPRESENTATION SHOULD NEVER EXCEED THE MINORITY'S REPRESENTATION BY MORE THAN ONE.

CONGRESS SHOULD CREATE A SINGLE, PRINCIPAL POINT OF OVERSIGHT AND REVIEW FOR HOMELAND SECURITY. THEY SHOULD CHOOSE ONE IN THE HOUSE AND ONE IN THE SENATE, AND THIS SHOULD BE A PERMANENT STANDING COMMITTEE WITH A NON-PARTISAN STAFF.

SINCE A CATASTROPHIC ATTACK COULD OCCUR WITH LITTLE OR NO NOTICE, WE SHOULD MINIMIZE THE DISRUPTION OF NATIONAL SECURITY POLICY MAKING DURING THE CHANGE OF ADMINISTRATIONS BY ACCELERATING THE PROCESS FOR NATIONAL SECURITY APPOINTMENTS.

BEFORE THE ELECTION, CANDIDATES SHOULD SUBMIT THE NAMES FOR THEIR PROSPECTIVE TRANSITION TEAMS TO THE FBI FOR CLEARANCE.

A PRESIDENT-ELECT SHOULD SUBMIT LISTS OF POSSIBLE CANDIDATES FOR NATIONAL SECURITY POSITIONS IMMEDIATELY AFTER THE ELECTION SO INVESTIGATIONS CAN BE COMPLETE BEFORE JANUARY 20.

THE SENATE, IN RETURN, SHOULD ADOPT SPECIAL RULES REQUIRING HEARINGS AND VOTES TO CONFIRM WITHIN 30 DAYS OF THEIR SUBMISSION.

THE OUTGOING ADMINISTRATION SHOULD PROVIDE THE PRESIDENT-ELECT AS SOON AS POSSIBLE AFTER ELECTION DAY WITH A CLASSIFIED, COMPARTMENTED LIST THAT CATALOGS SPECIFIC THREATS TO NATIONAL SECURITY.

OF ALL OUR RECOMMENDATIONS, STRENGTHENING CONGRESSIONAL OVERSIGHT MAY BE AMONG THE MOST DIFFICULT AND IMPORTANT. SO LONG AS OVERSIGHT IS GOVERNED BY CURRENT CONGRESSIONAL RULES AND RESOLUTIONS, WE BELIEVE THE AMERICAN PEOPLE WILL NOT GET THE SECURITY THEY WANT AND NEED.

Organizing America's Defenses in the United States

POSTSCRIPT

ON DECEMBER 5, 2005, THE 9/11 COMMISSION, AS ITS FINAL ACT, ISSUED A REPORT CARD RATING THE ACTIONS OF THE PRESIDENT AND CONGRESS IN THEIR RESPONSE TO THE COMMISSION'S FINDINGS AND RECOMMENDATIONS.
"THE RESULTS WERE DISMAL," WROTE COMMISSION MEMBER JAMES R. THOMPSON.
"PROGRESS IN MANY IMPORTANT AREAS HAS BEEN SLOW OR NONEXISTENT. WHILE THE TERRORISTS HAVE BEEN LEARNING AND ADAPTING, WE HAVE BEEN MOVING AT A BUREAUCRATIC CRAWL."
THAT REPORT CARD FOLLOWS...

HOMELAND SECURITY AND EMERGENCY RESPONSE

Radio spectrum for first responders	F/C*
Incident command system	C
Risk-based homeland security funds	F/A*
Critical infrastructure assessment	D
Private sector preparedness	C
National strategy for transportation security	C-
Airline passenger prescreening	F
Airline passenger explosive screening	C
Checked bag and cargo screening	D
Terrorist travel strategy	I
Comprehensive screening system	C
Biometric entry-exit screening system	B
International collaboration on borders and document security	D
Standardize secure identifications	B-

INTELLIGENCE AND CONGRESSIONAL REFORM

Director of national intelligence	B
National Counterterrorism Center	B
FBI national security workforce	C
New missions for CIA director	I
Incentives for information sharing	D
Governmentwide information sharing	D
Northern Command planning for homeland defense	B-
Full debate on Patriot Act	B
Privacy and civil liberties oversight board	D
Guidelines for government sharing of personal information	D
Intelligence oversight reform	D
Homeland security committees	B
Unclassified top-line intelligence budget	F
Security clearance reform	B

FOREIGN POLICY AND NONPROLIFERATION

Maximum effort to prevent terrorists from acquiring WMD	D
Afghanistan	B
Pakistan	C+
Saudi Arabia	D
Terrorist sanctuaries	B
Coalition strategy against Islamist terrorism	C
Coalition detention standards	F
Economic policies	B+
Terrorist financing	A-
Clear U.S. message abroad	C
International broadcasting	B
Scholarship, exchange, and library programs	D
Secular education in Muslim countries	D

* If pending legislation passes

ACKNOWLEDGMENTS

WE WOULD LIKE TO THANK ROGER BURLAGE FOR HIS STRONG BELIEF IN THIS PROJECT AND FOR HELPING US THROUGH THE DIFFICULTIES OF ITS COMPLETION. THIS BOOK COULD NOT HAVE BEEN REALIZED WITHOUT HIM. WE WOULD ALSO LIKE TO THANK THOMAS LEBIEN FOR HIS UNWAVERING APPRECIATION FOR WHAT WE HAVE TRIED TO DO AND FOR HIS INCREDIBLE GUIDANCE THROUGH EVERY STEP. HE HAS HELPED MAKE THIS BOOK MUCH MORE THAN WE COULD EVER HAVE ENVISIONED. AND WE MUST THANK BARRY GROSSMAN, THE COLORIST SUPREME, WHO STEPPED IN TO HELP US WITH HIS PALETTE IN THE FINAL MONTHS OF THIS ENDEAVOR. AND RICHARD STROM, FOR HIS EFFORTS THROUGHOUT IN COORDINATING OUR WORK AND KEEPING US ON SCHEDULE.

ERNIE COLÓN WOULD LIKE TO THANK RUTH ASHBY FOR HER HELP, PATIENCE, AND LOVE THROUGHOUT THIS COMPLEX AND REWARDING PROJECT. AND SID JACOBSON WOULD LIKE TO THANK SHURE LIFTON FOR HER SUPPORT, HER LOVE, AND HER SAINTLIKE PATIENCE.